Pensées

– A 40-Day Devotional for Pastors –

A JOURNEY PASTORAL COACHING RESOURCE

Pensées

– A 40-Day Devotional for Pastors –

D. Alan Baker

JPC
SHARING THE JOURNEY
JOURNEY PASTORAL COACHING

ISBN: 978-1-64719-999-9

This title is also available as an ebook at Booklocker.com.

Requests for information should be addressed to:
Journey Pastoral Coaching at journeypastoralcoaching.com

All Scripture quotations are from the English Standard Version (ESV) unless otherwise noted.

Printed on acid-free paper.

BookLocker.com, Inc.
2022

Cover design: Kayla Moon Designs
Design enquiries: kaylamoondesigns@gmail.com

First Edition

This book is dedicated to
the Journey Pastoral Coaching community,
the members and supporters
who make this mutual investment ministry
the life-giving community it is to so many.

Pensées

"pahn-say"

French
A collection of thoughts or reflections.

CONTENTS

ACKNOWLEDGEMENTS

My appreciation goes out to the Journey editorial team members who helped in the selection and editing of this material: Alicia Fierro, Allison Luna, Traci Crowder, Tyler Crowder, and Will Jones. My deepest thanks go out to my wife, Tricia, for sharing every step of this creative journey and every step of life's journey. Special thanks as well to Kayla Moon Designs for the cover design. Without all of your contributions, this project would not have been possible. You made it a joy.

I am grateful to the many authors and publishers who have not only kindly granted permission to cite their works but whose representatives have been so encouraging - different publishers and projects, but the same team and mission. Special appreciation goes out to the staff at BookLocker for their expertise and invaluable help in the publishing process.

Thank you to all the members of Journey Pastoral Coaching who have let me know throughout the year how much these daily devotions mean to you. Your encouragement was the original spark for this book.

Finally, my deepest thanks go out to all the people, those alive today and those with the Lord, whose passionate pursuit of Jesus has inspired me to live seeking the One who is worthy of all devotion, Jesus Christ.

"And I will give you shepherds after my own heart, who will feed you with knowledge and understanding."
Jeremiah 3.15

ONE THING

"One Thing I have asked from the Lord, that I shall seek: That I may dwell in the house of the Lord all the days of my life, To behold the beauty of the Lord And to meditate in His temple." Psalm 27.4

To be a pastor is to fulfill our Jeremiah 1.5 creation and calling. God knows us first as His children, but He has also formed us to be pastors. To adapt Jeremiah's phrasing, God knows us as pastors, His hand is on us as pastors, and He appoints us as pastors to His people.

It's not just what we do; it's who we are. Yes, we carry out the doing of pastoring, but only because of who we are. We are pastors: it is in the warp and woof of our individual creation and calling.

But to fulfill God's creation and calling, we must follow them in their natural order: by Him, to Him, and for Him. We are created by Him, first to be with Him, that, second, we might go out for Him. To have a healthy ministry, we must first see to the health of the minister. To grow sustainable pastoral ministries, we must first provide sustenance to the pastor. This means giving ourselves to our "first thing ministry": being with God. Again, before the doing, the being.

This natural order is seen in the earthly life of Jesus. The Gospels make it clear He could have preached to hundreds, if not thousands, every day of His public ministry. But He chose not to do so. Instead, His priority was time alone with God. In prayer, Jesus gave Himself over to the Father, yes, that He might minister to others, but first, that His being might be formed in the hands of the Father.

5

Even then, strong in His being, Jesus did not choose to preach daily to thousands but instead be with just twelve men. Jesus and The Twelve were very active in public ministry, but gave most of their time to just being together: walking Israel's roads, talking along the way, sharing meals, doing life. The overwhelming majority of Jesus' time with His disciples was "downtime," time spent not doing but being. It was in being with Jesus that the twelve became. When Jesus called The Twelve, He made His priorities clear for them:

> "Jesus went up on a mountainside and called to him those he wanted, and they came to him. He appointed twelve that they might be with him and that he might send them out to preach." Mark 3.13-14

Like most pastors, The Twelve may have been ready from the start to run in service for Jesus. But His first call was not to the work of the ministry. His first call was devotion to the Lord of the ministry. Before they could do, they needed to be and become. And meant they needed to give careful attention to their being.

They needed – we need - to develop a *One-Thing* ministry.

A ministry that begins in devotion to Jesus, a deepening love for Him that consistently and relentlessly draws us into quality and quantity time alone with Him – as it was with The Twelve. Not because we are required to do so, but because it is the deepest desire of our hearts. Because it is the greatest privilege of our lives.

The first call of The Twelve was to be with Jesus. Only as the Apostles were with Him could He then send them out in authority and power to minister in His name. These priorities remain in force today for those who would minister in Jesus' name.

To be a pastor is to live out our creation in devotion to our Creator, not only going out to work for Him but coming into Him for His re-creative work in us. We fulfill the purpose of our creation as we live, move, and have our being in the One who formed us. He continually shapes us as we invest time alone with Him – meditating on the Word of God and reflecting on the God of the Word. A life of contemplation.

To be a pastor is to live out our call in devotion to the One who not only called us to the ministry years ago but calls us every day to Himself. We fulfill the purpose of our call as we live, move, and have our being in Him. He renews our call as we invest time alone with Him – meditating on the Word of God and reflecting on the God of the Word. A life of contemplation.

A One-Thing ministry.

A pastor who contemplates? A pastor who intentionally stops ministry activity for God to cocoon with God, sitting over His Word and waiting in prayer? A pastor who longs to linger under the shadow of the wings of the Almighty, worshipping Him, listening quietly for His voice? A pastor who yearns to learn from Him and be refreshed by Him? Is there time and space in a 21st-century pastor's busy life for such indulgent "luxury?" Can the quiet invitation of God break through the noise of a life filled with the deafening calls to activity rather than prayer, CEO-ing rather than study, working for God rather than waiting and worshipping in His presence?

It is easy to hide from ourselves and our internal issues by keeping ourselves busy in the church. Fill our time with work for God in the church, and we don't have to face the work God wants to do in us – we can bury our doubts, questions, fears - and our sins - in the excuse of ministry for Him. The sad irony is that in hiding from ourselves, we hide from God. We shield ourselves from the Holy Spirit and the sanctifying work He could do in us if only we would draw near.

Yes, God desires to work through us in a world of need. But before He can work through us, He wants to, and must, work in us à la The Twelve in Mark 3. This is a work He will never do as we run through life working for Him, however good our intentions. God's refreshing is not found on the highways of our lives. It is waiting for us only in the rest areas – the secret places and hiding places, the spaces where we make Him our refuge and rest. His first requirement of us is not to live working for Him but waiting upon Him in contemplation, not because our ministry for God says we need it, but because our hearts say so.

> "I myself will see him
> with my own eyes—I, and not another.
> How my heart yearns within me!" Job 19.27

A *One-Thing* ministry.

No one is going to *give* you this time, Pastor, and no one is going to give you this life. You have to *take* this time; you have to *make* this life. You have to carve it out in your schedule and make it the most important element of your day. And this you will do when you carve out space in your heart for the most important assignment of your life: sitting quietly in God's presence, meditating on His Word, reflecting on Him in prayer, developing your soul in contemplation. You and those whom God has entrusted to you will soon note the mark of God's presence on your life. Everyone will be richer for it as you live to the heartbeat of your creation and calling.

Pastor, may the forty thoughts that follow serve you well, helping you develop a *One Thing* life and ministry.

— Day 1 —

FIRST THINGS FIRST

*"But we will devote ourselves to prayer and
to the ministry of the word." Acts 6.4*

PENSÉE: COURAGE
One of Jesus' most confrontational statements in the Gospels strikes
like a hammer: "You have heard it said, but I say.... "

Leadership theory says our first priority as pastors is leading. But
Jesus says it is following. We have often heard leadership experts tell
us our first priority is spending time with the members of our
leadership team, investing ourselves in them. But Jesus says our first
priority is time with God when He invests Himself in us.

In Acts 6, the first pastors of the church took a "You have heard
it said, but Jesus says" approach to pastoring. They freed themselves
of others' ideas about pastoral priorities. They understood they served
their people best as they ordered their ministries by God's priorities.

They would be pastors who gave themselves first to prayer and
the Word. As pastors, they would focus on the spiritual needs of the
church while appointing others to focus on the material needs. This
did not devalue the people. Instead, it elevated them as the pastors set
the needs of the people under the lordship of God. As the pastors and
people followed God and His priorities, He would faithfully provide.
The apostle-pastors served the people well when they prayerfully

9

concluded that nothing could come before their devotion to prayer and the Word.

The way of the Acts 6 pastors has been lost by many in our time. This life path for pastors is overgrown with the weeds of our professional approach. Business practices rule the church and a managerial mindset has replaced a pastoral *heartset*. Giving ourselves to prayer and the Word is a foreign concept for many in pastoral ministry today, busy managing organizations and answering the call of endless to-do lists. We are eager learners of leadership techniques but truant students in the disciplined study of God's Word – how many sermons are not the product of our daily study but a search engine. We are experts in management but novices in prayer, unable to watch and pray for an hour with Him who is our very life.

The consequences of pastors not giving themselves to prayer and the Word are now evident in the American church (and culture). Study after study reveals a church weak in doctrine and discipleship.

Pastor, it's time we get back to our call and commission, back to a life of devotion to Jesus Christ. It's time to get back on our knees, back in The Book, and back to proclaiming the Word in the fire we receive there as we meet with God.

> *"Nothing is more needed among preachers today than that we should have the courage to shake ourselves free from the thousand and one trivialities in which we are asked to waste our time and strength, and resolutely return to the apostolic ideal which made necessary the office of the pastorate. We will continue steadfastly in prayer, and in the ministry of the Word." G. Campbell Morgan*[1]

---

[1] Taken from *This Was His Faith: The Expository Letters of G. Campbell Morgan*, edited by Jill Morgan (Westwood: Fleming Revell, 1952). Used by permission.

— Day 2 —

DROUGHT FREE

"Two are better than one, because they have a good reward for their toil. For if they fall, one will lift up his fellow. But woe to him who is alone when he falls and has not another to lift him up! Again, if two lie together, they keep warm, but how can one keep warm alone? And though a man might prevail against one who is alone, two will withstand him— a threefold cord is not quickly broken." Ecclesiastes 4.9-12

PENSÉE: RELATIONSHIPS

In conversations with pastors of all ages, I often hear this troubling statement: "I feel alone." Sadly, I hear it far too often from those who lead what we call faith "communities." Surrounded by people, many shepherds feel isolated.

"Who are you walking with in a meaningful way?" I ask. "No one," comes the flat response.

"Who are you talking with about the issues of your life?" Again, they respond, "No one."

"Why not?" I ask. "I don't know," comes the almost machine-like answer. It's an experience known by too many: surveys continue to find that the overwhelming majority of pastors report having no close friends. None. Not one.

The number one killer of ministers is isolation. And with the minister, the ministry often dies as well. We make every excuse we can think of to isolate: we're too busy, too tired, it's a strange season (for twenty years!?), we're introverts, personality tests indicate we are IXJZ types, no one cares about us, etc.

And we're all too ready to believe these lies. All the while knowing our actions are placing the hands of isolation around our necks in an ever tightening death hold. Deep down, we know it.

A man dying of thirst in the desert has but one thought: water. And he is willing to do whatever he must do to get it. In stark contrast, too often, pastors dying of isolation have just one thought, one solution: more isolation. And they're willing to die for it. It's heartbreaking.

Pastor, let's make a vow today. Let's make a vow to break the cycle of death and end the drought of relationships in our lives forever. Reach out to someone near you. Reach out for your sake. Reach out for the sake of that person; who knows, he or she might be just as lonely as you. Talk together. Laugh together. Cry together. Pray together. Talk to your pastoral coach or mentor. Call a peer in your coaching community or circle of friends. Make a second, third, and even fourth call. Call and talk for an hour or for even five minutes of prayer together. Get coffee with a colleague in your town.

Let's end the drought of relationships among pastors for good. For good in more than one way. As we do so, the living waters of Jesus will flow to us and through us in satisfying soul-refreshing.

> *"He prayed for the end of a different type of drought. He asked God, 'Please end the drought of relationships.'"* Chris Maxwell[2]

---

[2] Taken from *Pause for Pastors* by Chris Maxwell. (Travelers Rest, SC: True Potential Inc., 2014) p.64. chrismaxwell.me. Used by permission.

— *Day 3* —

THE SAME GRACE

*"Paul, an apostle of Christ Jesus by command of God our Savior and of
Christ Jesus our hope. To Timothy, my true child in the faith:
grace, mercy, and peace from God the Father and
Christ Jesus our Lord." I Timothy 1.1-2*

PENSÉE: GRACE
Do you preach grace, Pastor? And do you preach it not only to others
but to yourself?

Grace is what brought Jesus into the world, angels announcing
His coming as "Good News": "God News," for all people. Grace is
the God News that, though we are sinners, we can be reconciled to
God. Grace promised in a manger. Grace delivered on a Cross.

Let us preach that grace – passionately, tenderly, even urgently.
Let us extend to people God's promise that whatever they have done,
they can come home to Him.

Don't make the mistake of assuming this offer of grace means
overlooking sin. Not at all! How can it be grace unless the subject is
also sin! If we are sin-free, we do not need grace, but because we are
born sinners and are sinners saved by grace, we need grace not only
at salvation but all the days of our salvation until we meet the Savior.
Pastor, preach grace.

But don't only preach it in word. Preach it in heart and deed. How? First, be gracious, allowing God's grace to flow through you to others. Second, be grateful, letting God's praise flow from your heart to His. A gracious and grateful life is the evidence of grace at work in us.

Finally, let grace work in you. Let the grace you preach to others be your own possession and ongoing experience. Don't live only as a vessel of grace to others, but let that grace work in you. Let it comfort you when you are hurting. Let it forgive and cleanse you when you sin. Let it give you hope when you see no future. Let it convince you of God's love when you would condemn yourself for your past. Even more for your present.

Over the years, if you will let it, grace will be your best friend. And what a wonderful friend it is. It will continually identify your sins, not to condemn but to convict, cut away, and give you life in its place. God's grace will go to the same sins it has dealt with dozens of times and deal with them still again, because God is relentlessly working to renew you in Jesus, even in in the most challenging areas of your heart. By God's grace, even in these places, Christ will reign!

Finally, grace is not about becoming comfortable with sin. It is about becoming comfortable with God's process of sanctification. Yes, you and I sin, but no, we are not failures; we are children of God, and our loving Heavenly Father is disciplining us for our good.

Over the years, as grace does its work, we come to embrace it for its sanctifying and satisfying work. We are sinners saved by grace, in constant need of a Savior. And it's ok. More than that, it's a wonder. It's good news! It's Immanuel, God with us.

"A pastor needs the same grace he offers his people. He needs the same Gospel." Le Prédicateur[3]

---

[3] Journey Pastoral Coaching, Copyright © 2021

— *Day 4* —

GOD'S WORK, GOD'S SUPPLY

"And my God will supply every need of yours according to his riches in glory in Christ Jesus. To our God and Father be glory forever and ever. Amen." Philippians 4.19-20

PENSÉE: PROVISION

This is a challenging thought, one that's easy to talk about in college and seminary but challenging to walk as we pastor our churches.

I remember moving into the church of my dreams, dreams that quickly turned into a nightmare. I remember that first Monday when the bank vice-president told me the church was so far behind in its mortgage we could never catch up - why shouldn't he take possession of our building? I remember my first Tuesday when I found a file folder, inches thick, filled with past due bills.

I remember the businesses that would no longer accept our church checks. I remember the Sunday a visitor told me, regretfully, that he had to name our church as co-defendants in a lawsuit for hundreds of thousands of dollars for actions taken before I was pastor. I remember the weekly expenses that doubled our weekly income for the first few months of our pastorate.

I remember cutting my pay and telling the board of my decision. I remember my wife, eight-months pregnant, taking over the direction of our church daycare, receiving no salary as she worked twelve-hour days, taking just two days off when she gave birth to our first child.

I remember the empty seats in the sanctuary, the empty children's church and nursery. I remember a congregation that had been through two devastating splits and was unsure of its future.

I remember it all.

I remember telling our people of our situation (not all of it). I remember telling them my wife and I would lead the way in sacrifice and giving - we had committed to giving God not ten percent of our income but fifteen percent. We invited the church to join us in investing in our future: if we had a heart to give, God would bless. I remember telling them the church had not supported any of its twenty-six missionaries for several years. We were going to correct that. My wife and I would bring an offering for missions every week. We invited our people to do the same: if we kept our word to God, He would meet our needs.

I remember God meeting me every Saturday night as I lay before Him in the altar, calling on Him to build His church because I surely could not do it. I remember when God came down, powerfully meeting us every service – in worship, in the Word, and in the altars.

I remember the week God even sent in support from another state, friends who did not know our situation, but had felt prompted to give. I didn't deposit that check until I first took it to church on Sunday and held it up for my people to see! Our church had responded to God, and He was responding yet again with His blessing!

Day by day, we learned that because it is God's church, He *will* supply our needs according to His riches in Christ Jesus.

> *"Depend on it! God's work done in God's way will never lack God's supply."* *Hudson Taylor*[4]

---

[4] Hudson Taylor, from his personal journal. Public domain.

— Day 5 —

TRANSFORMATIONAL MINISTRY

Be on guard for yourselves and for all the flock, among which the Holy Spirit has made you overseers, to shepherd the church of God which He purchased with His own blood. Acts 20.28

PENSÉE: FOCUS

Pastor, we are not marketers, dealers, performers, or magicians. Our calling and task are not to attract, sell, impress, or amaze.

We are shepherds. Our calling and task are to tend sheep. More precisely, tend their souls. Night and day, 24/7, in sunshine and rain, we maintain our vigil, watching over those whom God has entrusted to us as their soul-shepherds (Hebrews 13.17).

We sit on hillsides under star-filled skies, and we watch, one eye on the sheep and one eye scanning the terrain for those who would do them harm. We guide the sheep to still waters and green pastures. We lead them in paths of righteousness. We comfort them with a rod and staff of protection. We keep a table of feasting prepared for them, even in the presence of their enemies. We anoint them with oil. Through us and our Spirit-empowered ministry, the Great Good Shepherd restores their souls.

And He transforms their souls. In service to Jesus and by the power of the Holy Spirit, our shepherding not only restores but transforms. The spiritual food and water we give them, the paths on

17

which we lead them, the rod and staff of comfort we carry, the feasting on the good things of God, and the oil we use to anoint them do far more than heal the soul from past weariness and harm. These transform, adding muscle to their souls, taking them from strength to strength and from glory to glory.

Pastor, God uses the work you do every day to transform lives. You can depend on it. You must.

This is the promise and guarantee of the Great Good Shepherd you serve in leading His flock. Don't give in to the temptation to join the marketers, dealers, performers, and magicians. Their fame will last as long as they are able to amaze and out-entertain the next hireling who comes along. But your legacy will live on for eternity in the lives of those who, in this world and the world to come, say to you, "Thank you for watching over my soul so faithfully. Thank you for being my pastor."

> *"Don't focus on what astonishes, but rather on what transforms." José Luis Navajo,*[5]

---

[5] Taken from *Mondays With My Old Pastor* by José Luis Navajo. (Nashville: Thomas Nelson 2012). p.11. thomasnelson.com. Used by permission.

— Day 6 —

FOR THE LONG HAUL

"He has made everything beautiful in its time. Also, he has put eternity into man's heart, yet so that he cannot find out what God has done from the beginning to the end." Ecclesiastes 3.11

PENSÉE: ENDURANCE
Pastor, because the years can seem to pass by without noticeable results - day after day after seemingly unchanging days - we can easily question our abilities and ourselves. Where is the evidence of our effectiveness for Jesus? Where is the change in people's lives? Where is the spiritual growth? Just how is the church coming into the unity of Christ that Paul writes about in his letters? What real difference do our days as pastors make in the local churches we pastor, much less in the grand scheme of things?

I have two wonderful daughters. Each of them is a delight to me in her own way. Both are now grown, married, and have families of their own. I thank God for this. To see them happily married, serving God, and teaching their children to serve Jesus is a joy beyond words.

But what I want to know is how did this happen? Where did the time go? And how did the two little girls in my memory become these strong and capable women whom I not only love as my daughters but so respect as people?

It happened one day at a time. One sunrise and sunset at a time. One conversation at a time. One book at a time. One story at a time. One school day at a time. One trip to the zoo at a time. One driving lesson at a time. One hug at a time. One prayer at a time.

It happened over many years of one days. It happened over a too-quickly passed season of one moments.

If my wife and I had tried to rush the process, requiring them to be young women when they were still little girls, we would have harmed them. If we had tried to hold onto little girls when they were becoming young women, the harm would have been much the same. We had to let them, and help them, grow one day at a time, under the loving hand of the Heavenly Father.

Our little girls became strong women as their mother and I did what all God-fearing and loving parents do: we loved them and led them one day at a time, trusting the Lord who makes all things beautiful in their time to bring them into their full individual beauty and strength.

Pastor, your Lord is the God who makes all things beautiful in their time. Even your church. How do I know this? Because it is His church. And as much as I care for my daughters, my love for them cannot begin to compare to God's love for your church. Patience, Pastor. And, yes, lots of love and prayer and teaching and more. But above all, patience. God is making all things beautiful in their time.

> *"One of the most important things to know about pastoring is that the long-term results are never fully known until years and years have passed by." Gordon MacDonald*[6]

---

[6] Taken from *Going Deep* by Gordon MacDonald, (Nashville: Thomas Nelson, 2011). p.227. Used by permission.

— Day 7 —

PEBBLES

Have this mind among yourselves, which is yours in Christ Jesus, who, though he was in the form of God, did not count equality with God a thing to be grasped, but emptied himself, by taking the form of a servant, being born in the likeness of men. And being found in human form, he humbled himself by becoming obedient to the point of death, even death on a cross. Therefore, God has highly exalted him and bestowed on him the name that is above every name, so that at the name of Jesus every knee should bow, in heaven and on earth and under the earth, and every tongue confess that Jesus Christ is Lord, to the glory of God, the Father. Philippians 2.5-11

PENSÉE: CONTENTMENT

Who notices pebbles? We walk past them every day and give them little or no notice.

But take a pebble to a tranquil pond and toss it onto the transparent and seamless sheet of its surface. And then watch as an amazing occurrence takes place. The casting of this small, insignificant pebble into the water affects the entire pond. As it strikes one small point of the water's surface, it instantly disappears, leaving passersby to wonder what caused the stirring that now slowly and steadily works its way in wave after wave to the water's edge.

But the question of what caused the stirring is a secondary one. What is significant is not the pebble. What is significant is the stirring taking place across the entire pond.

21

I am only a pebble. But I am God's pebble.

He chooses my time and place. He decides if I am to be noticed or passed by unseen. He determines the pond, great or small, into which He casts me. But none of this matters to me, for I am His, formed by Him and for Him, to serve His higher purposes. This is all I desire and more.

I am God's pebble. And I am content in this marvelous truth and ministry.

"Pastors are God's pebbles." Le Prédicateur[7]

---

[7] Journey Pastoral Coaching, Copyright © 2021

— Day 8 —

SHEPHERD OF SOULS

*"Obey your leaders and submit to them, for they are keeping watch over
your souls, as those who will have to give an account. Let them do this with
joy and not with groaning, for that would be of no advantage to you."*
Hebrews 13.17

PENSÉE: HABITUS
Pastor, you and I are undershepherds of Jesus Christ. In His name, we
watch over people's souls - not just over people, but over their souls.
And because of this, one day we will give an account to God of our
watch care, a thought that should keep us all on our knees.

Just this week, I read a book on pastoring, one filled with
technique after technique on how a pastor can add people to his
church. Its subject was not how to see people come to Christ, but to
the church you pastor – how to attract people, give them great
experiences, and make them want to stay in your church. But it said
very little on how to shepherd souls or keep watch over them. Even
more concerning, it said next-to-nothing on developing the character
and heart of a shepherd. The writer sees the church as just an
organization and people as a means to an end: the leader's success.

Thank God the Great Good Shepherd sees the Church as
something of far greater value. He sees it as His people, the sheep of
His pasture (Psalm 100.3), and every person in the church as an

23

immortal soul, a child of God. Thank God He personally sees you, knows you, and loves you. And because He loves you, he is not "techniquing" you into doing what makes the church merely look good, but He is working all things together for good, including yours.

Thank God His activity in your life is not a collection of techniques designed to manipulate you but is the outflow of His being, working in you to help your soul grow in health. His activity in your life is first that of a Father in the life of His child. And then it is that of a Shepherd in the life of you, His undershepherd. As your son-and-shepherd soul prospers in Him, God will use you to immerse souls in your church in His character and identity, to the glory of God, the health of your people, and the salvation of a lost world.

Be in Jesus today, Pastor. Be who God created you and called you to be. Then be a pastor to your people, helping them be all God created and called them to be. In following the Great Good Shepherd this way, you and your people can know all God has for you.

By the way, that book on successful pastoring? Midway through it, the author wrote about healthy reading, admonishing pastors not to waste their time on unhelpful books. His counsel was that once a pastor sees a book isn't worth his time, the pastor shouldn't waste his time. He should close the book and be done with it. I took his advice.

> *"Remember you are a shepherd of souls. This is not just a job or a vocation; this is a habitus. Remember that what you do flows from who you are. And as you develop that character and identity of a shepherd it colors the way you look at the sheep and interact with them. Rather than a two-stage thinking/doing process, your pastoral response becomes increasingly reflexive and instinctive." Harold Senkbeil*[8]

---

[8] Taken from *The Care of Souls* by Harold Senkbeil. (Bellingham: Lexham Press, 2019), p.70. Used by permission.

— Day 9 —

SEASONS

"For everything there is a season,
and a time for every matter under heaven:
a time to be born, and a time to die;
a time to plant, and a time to pluck up what is planted.
Ecclesiastes 3.1-2

PENSÉE: RHYTHMS

As an undershepherd of the Great Good Shepherd, my work assignment is to recognize what God is doing and join Him in doing it. For everything in my life and ministry, there is a season, a harvest for which God is planning and working. I want to join Him in that work so the results He desires can be as great as possible.

As I take on this assignment, I must understand that God's first work is in me: forming me in the image of His Son. Through cycles of sowing, watering, cultivating, and, yes, pruning, God is ever working to conform me to the image of His Son, Jesus Christ. My priority is joining Him in this work, beginning with consistently giving myself to the Word and prayer. Only as I am an ongoing work in the hands of God am I prepared to join Him in the work He is doing in His church and world.

But as you give yourself to the work of God in and through you, Pastor, it is essential you understand God's seasons, and work in rhythm with them - seasons of sowing and reaping, waiting and working, seasons of our youth and later years. Each season holds its own life-giving rhythms. How vital it is we step in time with those rhythms so the work of God in and through our lives in each season might be fruitful. So, He might make all things beautiful in their time.

People feel the love of God in the spring seasons of life as we experience being born again, personal revival, or as God's creation in us is renewed. We know His joy in the warm months of our full life summers, fruitfulness and contentment in the harvest season of fall. But where is God in the winter seasons of life? Why can He seem so far away when life becomes cold? Where is the rhythm of the Spirit in the hard days of our spiritual winters? Are the winters of our lives really destined to be seasons of only cold isolation?

No, even in life's winters, God is at work in the world. Even when your world seems lifeless and cold, He is at work in you and the people you pastor. Look for it! Scan the horizons of your life! Think on what wonders He is even now working in and through you!

As a pastor, you help others navigate these seasons. You help them recognize life's rhythms and then develop the life-giving spiritual disciplines needed to navigate them as Spirit-led disciples.

But, Pastor, how can you help others grow in spiritual disciplines if you do not live in them yourself? How can you help others walk in step with the Spirit if you don't live in the daily rhythm of Word and prayer? The weekly rhythm of Sabbath? The rhythms of the calendar that speak to us of God's work in us? Let's not forget the changing rhythms of life that come in our youth and later years.

How vital it is we work in rhythm with every season. Only then will we be able to thrive in those seasons, be they the energetic days of our springs or the quieting days of our winters.

Pastor, let's learn to recognize the seasons of our lives and ministries. Let's learn the rhythms of each season: our springs, summers, falls, and even winters. Let's discover what God is doing in each of these times and join Him in doing it. To help us in this work, let's find His rhythm for each day, week, and season. And then, as we do, let's dance in love, joy, and peace to His songs even as we anticipate seasons to come. Because we know who holds all the seasons of life, who knows what blessings the next season holds? Who knows what harvest it will yield?

"Inappropriate, anxiety driven, fear driven work would only interfere with and distract from what's God was already doing. My "work" assignment was to pay more attention to what God does than what I do, and then to find, and guide others to find, the daily, weekly, yearly rhythms that would get this awareness into our bones. Holy Saturday for a start. And then Sabbath keeping. Staying in touch with people in despair, knowing them by name, and waiting for resurrection." Eugene H. Peterson[9]

---

[9] Taken from *The Pastor: A Memoir* by Eugene Peterson. (San Francisco: HarperOne, 2012), p.58. harperone.com. Used by permission.

— *Day 10* —

MUTUAL INVESTMENT MINISTRY

*"And they devoted themselves to the apostles' teaching and the fellowship,
to the breaking of bread and the prayers. And awe came upon every soul,
and many wonders and signs were being done through the apostles.
And all who believed were together and had all things in common.
And they were selling their possessions and belongings and distributing
the proceeds to all, as any had need. And day by day, attending the temple
together and breaking bread in their homes, they received their food
with glad and generous hearts." Acts 2.42-47*

PENSÉE: COMMUNITY

A professor at a Midwestern university explained to a Christian friend
why he was not a follower of Jesus. He said he would be convinced
of Christ's reality if the church would be what it claims to be. No, he
did not charge hypocrisy; he craved community. He said if he saw
real community in Christ's "body," he would believe in the reality of
the Head. He could not believe in the Head, Jesus, because, he said,
he had never seen His body. His reason for refusing Jesus Christ:

"The church has never learned the secret of community."

Fault this man's lack of faith if you want, but his critique stings
with accuracy: "If there is no community in the "body of Christ," how
can there be a life-giving head, Jesus Christ?"

29

If we lack community, what can we do to restore it and see it grow? How can the life of Jesus become our shared Acts 2 life?

An answer: what if we could imagine a place where ministers of all kinds come together to learn and practice community so they could then lead in the practice of community among believers everywhere? A community so tangible it transcends space and time, able to thrive in the same room or separated by a thousand miles? A community so vibrant that members come not to be served, but to serve – actually joining because they are looking for ways to encourage, support, challenge, and strengthen others? A community so strong it soul-level sorrows with those who sorrow and soul-level rejoices with those who rejoice? And yes, a community that can even hear the confession of those who have sinned and, in empathy, see them healed (James 5.16)? A community so transformational that it flows like water in daily redemption through each member to each member – *and then to their churches?*

Can you imagine such a community?

Forgive the dreams of an "old man," but I can. Acts 2 tells me the Holy Spirit will give old men dreams. These dreams shall not only captivate them in meaningless daydreams, but captivate and take flight in the lives of others who are open to all the Holy Spirit has for us, The Community of Christ, His Body. This is the way.

> *Although I have much to be grateful for as I look back over my life, I also have many regrets. I have failed many times, and I would do many things differently... I would give more attention to fellowship with other Christians, who could teach me and encourage me and even rebuke me when necessary. Billy Graham.*[10]

---

[10] ©2016 Billy Graham Evangelistic Association. Charlotte, NC. All rights reserved. billygraham.org. Used by permission.

— Day 11 —

THE AUDIENCE OF ONE

"Now when they saw the boldness of Peter and John, and perceived that they were uneducated, common men, they were astonished. And they recognized that they had been with Jesus." Acts 4.13

PENSÉE: FOCUS

Have you noticed how divided our pastoral focus can become? We pay attention to so many things but fix our gaze on only a few, maybe none at all.

As a result, it's off to races, running here and there, taking care of this project and propping up that program, putting out a wildfire, and restarting a needed fire that went out. At the end of the day, we lay our heads on the pillow, not just exhausted but without rest. We've chased the to-do list and its commands all day long but satisfied none. Least of all, ourselves. Too many tasks. Too little time. We would never admit this, but too many masters.

One of my daughters was in high school and college theatre. She was an exceptionally talented actress. In one role, she so immersed herself in her stage character that I almost didn't recognize her, though she was only feet away from me. Her success in her performance was not in the camouflage of heavy make-up or costuming but in her ability to become the character in essence.

31

The keys? There were two. First, in preparing and performing, she did not focus on pleasing the hundreds of people who would see her and judge her according to their expectations. Instead, she focused her full attention on immersing herself in the character the writer-director had created.

Second, once she was fully immersed in the heart and head of the character, she focused her attention on the writer-director and his instructions in rehearsals as she worked to bring that character to life. She focused on *being* the character the writer-director had written, knowing that the *doing* would naturally flow from this. Yes, an audience was in the seats, but meeting its expectations was not her focus. Her focus was on the writer-director and satisfying him. Performing before hundreds, she had an audience of only one. Only one. At the end of each performance, she had the applause of her grateful audience. But more significant to her, she had the "well done" of her proud writer-director.

Pastor, our first focus is that of being conformed to the character of Jesus. This happens as we daily invite the Holy Spirit to transform us through the Script(ures). Focused on being conformed to the character of Jesus, we focus our full attention on Him, the Writer-Director, intent on following His instructions.

Yes, we know people are watching as we play our part. But our motivation does not come from meeting their expectations. Our motivation is single-minded: the Creator-Writer of our life's story. We know as we focus on being conformed to the character of Christ, the doing will naturally follow. "Performing" before hundreds or a handful, we have an audience of only one. At the end of each sermon, Sunday, or a lifetime of service, we may have the appreciation of a grateful congregation. But more importantly, we will have the "well done" of our proud Writer-Director. Our audience of One.

"True success for the pastor is a life focused on The Audience of One. It is to live as concentrated on God as a young man who, on one knee, has only one desire and question for the one earthly love of his life." Le Prédicateur[11]

---

[11] Journey Pastoral Coaching, Copyright © 2021

— *Day 12* —

THE WEIGHT OF GLORY

"And being found in human form, he humbled himself by becoming obedient to the point of death, even death on a cross." Philippians 2.8

PENSÉE: THE CROSS

Pastor, do you know older ministers who walk in the abundant life of Jesus? Those on whom rests a presence, a depth, a "weight of glory?"

Engrave this word in stone: they have spent a lifetime abiding hard by the Cross.

Over a lifetime of ministry, there were for these "weight of glory" ministers no attraction to the latest and greatest ministry fad. The fascination was with the Cross, and its crucified and risen Savior.

There was no craving to climb ladders of influence: the only yearning was a Cross, and its crucified and risen Savior.

There was no thrill in impressing leaders or building a group of followers: the only wonder to seek was a Cross, and its crucified and risen Savior.

These pastors walk in the life of the empty tomb today because they have lived a lifetime with their hearts fixed on the Cross and its Crucified Christ.

Pastor, where is the Cross in your life? Yes, where is it in your ministry, but first, where is it in your life? Are you abiding hard by the Cross in your own life or only passing by it from time to time when the weight of ministry presses too heavily on your shoulders?

Where are the wounds of the crucified Christ in your life? Yes, where are they in your ministry, but where are they in your life? Are you giving yourself to searching the mysteries of the wounds of the Son of God slain for you or only using them as preaching themes? Do you still stand in awestruck gratitude at the terrible price Jesus paid for your sins? Do you still wonder at the grace of God in your life?

The older minister on whom the weight of glory so preciously and powerfully rests still wonders at grace so amazing. After a lifetime of service, he has never gotten over his awe at the sacrifice of Jesus for him. And he doesn't want to do so.

Pastor, would you walk in those depths with God in your later years? Your journey into His depths commences today. It begins as you turn away from chasing fads, attracting a following, or seeking to impress others. It begins as you turn to the way known by "weight of glory" disciples for more than two millennia: abiding hard by the Cross, following its crucified and risen Savior with everything you have within you.

Let us stop our search for the magic pill of significant influence or instant spirituality and look again to the wounds that not only killed death for us over two thousand years ago but give us life today! Let us be pastors with only one passion: the crucified and risen Savior!

> *"Abide hard by the Cross and search the mysteries of His wounds." Charles Spurgeon*[12]

---

[12] Taken from *Morning and Evening* by Charles Spurgeon. Public domain.

— Day 13 —

AMERICAN IDOLATRY

"Jesus, ... rose from supper. He laid aside his outer garments, and taking a towel, tied it around his waist. Then he poured water into a basin and began to wash the disciples' feet and to wipe them with the towel that was wrapped around him." John 13.5

PENSÉE: WORSHIP

I remember returning to the United States after our family's second term of missionary service in Europe.

As we made our way through the airport in Washington D.C., I was surprised, even shocked, at the many signs advertising something called "American Idol." I had no idea what this was and had no time to find out as we hurried to make our next flight. I later learned this was the latest must-watch TV show. America couldn't wait to bow before their TV sets each week to watch American Idol. No one seemed bothered by the title either: "C'mon, it's just a show title. It doesn't mean anything!"

But, as many are realizing, words mean things. Today, we are a nation in full-blown idolatry, idols of every kind, particularly celebrity. People will do anything to claim the media spotlight and their fleeting moment of fame, i.e., self-idolatry.

Even in the church.

When was the last time you heard someone say they attend ABC Church because of its discipleship or prayer ministry? When was the last time you heard someone say they attend XYZ Church because Pastor JZ rocks or their worship team is awesome?

American Idol, meet American Church Idol.

As a result, the American church is reaping what we have sown: our "chief-among-celebrities" ministry model is insufficient to sustain the church, much less strengthen it. People are heading for the doors and not coming back. Our celebrity entertainers just aren't as good as the celebrity entertainers of the world. Reducing our ministry to celebrity, we have reduced the Church to a club, one among many options for shoppers of religious and spiritual "experiences."

And rather than go back to the ancient wells - seeking the face of God with Book of Acts intensity - we wonder how we can tweak our techniques to make our religious programming more intense, comfortable, or attractive than the latest must-see church everyone is now attending. Until the next bigger-and-better American Church Idol launches large across town. Our prayer rooms are empty, but our concerts-as-church are crowded. Our discipleship is dead, but our celebrity pulpits are full. The presence of God may not be evident, but not to worry: we've got a hip pastor and an awesome worship team that just won't quit.

One ordinary pastor raises his head and heart from the altar long enough to rock our self-focused ministries and cast down our American idolatry with this rock-the-house thought:

> *"Some churches have converted their altars into stages and that is a real problem. On a stage is where celebrities shine; on an altar is where God's presence comes down. The two are incompatible; we will have to choose: human celebrities or godly impact." José Luis Navajo*[13]

---

[13] Navajo, p.22.

— Day 14 —

SNEAK ATTACK

"For the weapons of our warfare are not of the flesh but have divine power to destroy strongholds." II Corinthians 10.4

PENSÉE: SPIRITUAL WARFARE
Consider this provocative thought, Pastor:

"For all the skirmishes we get involved in as pastors, I've come to believe we make it harder on ourselves because we're fighting the wrong enemy with the wrong tactics and the wrong weapons."

A provocative thought. So quick am I to take up weapons of the flesh to fight what are, in fact, spiritual battles. Yes, even battles that take place in our churches. Just because we are sons and daughters of God, a part of the church of Jesus Christ, you and I are not free from demonic attack. Read the apostle Paul's letters from the front lines for more on this.

And then, when someone sounds a call to respond with spiritual warfare, we catch the side glances of those who have "progressed" beyond such primitive faith. We see the smirks. Meanwhile, hell smiles and signals its forces: "Battle tactic 111 working as planned."

I remember attending a meeting of thousands of ministers from around the world. In one plenary session, a well-known leader declared with great assurance the power of God to save, heal, and deliver. It was obvious he was absolutely convinced of the truth of his message, not as only a denominational doctrine, but as his breath and blood experience with the truth.

He was preaching truth on fire! He told the story of his mother who, when she heard of a serious need, would enter her bedroom, close the door, get on her knees before God and not come out until she had "broken through." It wasn't just a great story from the past. It wasn't just a powerful reminder of the promises of God. It was a call to action, a call to run to the battle with the weapons of warfare God has supplied.

There were those who smiled like knowing sophisticates at the simplistic faith of these old-time believers who didn't have the benefit of the education believers now enjoy.

But the one thing they couldn't do in their smugness was refute either the story or the truth it demonstrated:

"For the weapons of our warfare are not of the flesh but have divine power to destroy strongholds." II Corinthians 10.4

Consider well the Prayer of Consecration for new local bishops, recorded in the Canons of Hippolytus [2nd-Century AD]:

"Grant unto him, O Lord,... the power to break all the chains of the evil power of the demons, to cure all the sick, and speedily to subdue Satan beneath his feet."

Pastor, the weapons of your warfare are not of the flesh, but they do have divine power to destroy strongholds! You and I have our degrees, and they have their rightful place in our lives and ministries. But in the great battle between the kingdoms of light and darkness, they have no standing nor power. It is not by might, nor by power, but by HIS Spirit, the Lord of Hosts!

Stand in that might! Better still, kneel in that might until you see that power breaking through in your life, ministry, and church. And then advance, in Jesus' mighty name!

> *"For all the skirmishes we get involved in as pastors, I've come to believe that we make it harder on ourselves because we're fighting the wrong enemy with the wrong tactics and the wrong weapons. It doesn't help much that while we get a lot of training in leadership strategies and conflict management, we receive precious little instruction in spiritual warfare. I think that's why a lot of pastors are sitting ducks in ministry; they're flying blind and don't grasp what they're really up against. No wonder so many are so highly stressed and so often on the brink of burnout." Harold Senkbeil[14]*

---

[14] Senkbeil, p.195.

— Day 15 —

FORWARD & BACKWARD

*"Grace and peace be yours in abundance through the knowledge of God
and of Jesus our Lord. His divine power has given us everything we need
for a godly life through our knowledge of him who called us by his own
glory and goodness. Through these he has given us his very great and
precious promises, so that through them you may participate in the divine
nature, having escaped the corruption in the world caused by evil desires."*
II Peter 1.2-4

PENSÉE: TRUST

In his second letter, the Apostle Peter reminds believers of a life-
changing truth: God has given us many precious and powerful
promises (II Peter 1.3-4).

Among them is the open door to His glory and excellence, His
divine nature, and experiencing the power of God that gives all things
pertaining to life and godliness. Peter does not even begin to exhaust
the many promises of God described for us from Genesis to
Revelation. In His letter, he simply echoes other biblical writers in
urging us to activate our confidence in God and "faith forward" to
possess these promises.

But in verse 2, Peter reminds us of an even more precious and
powerful truth: God has given us something to be treasured even
more than His promises. He has given us Himself, the God of
promise. Because we know Him, all-encompassing grace and peace

are ours in abundance. It is a promise the Apostle Peter offers in his first letter: "Though you have not seen him, you love him. Though you do not now see him, you believe in him and rejoice with joy that is inexpressible and filled with glory, obtaining the outcome of your faith, the salvation of your souls" (I Peter 1. 8-9). He echoes the greatest of all promises given to us in scripture: The Sovereign God is our loving Father, and we are His people. Whatever we face in life, yes, we can *faith forward* into the promises of God, but even more, we can *fall back* into Him, trusting Him to guide and provide.

Though heaven and earth pass away, God's Word, including His promises, will remain (Matthew 24.25). His Word, including His promises, will accomplish anything and everything He sends it to do (Isaiah 55.11). We can faith forward into the promises of God.

And don't miss this, Pastor: the God who called you is worthy of your trust - He is faithful and true. He promises to never forsake those who seek Him, those who place their trust in Him (Psalm 9.10). Even when we face the impossible, we can trust in the all-things-are-possible God: "By faith, Sarah herself received power to conceive, even when she was past the age since she considered him faithful who had promised (Hebrews 11.11). We can trust back into the God of promise.

Know today that the promises of God are as sure and true as the One who gives them.

Pastor, today and every day, God is urging you to activate your faith in pressing forward to possess the promise of God. He's inviting you to trust back into the arms of the God of promise.

"Pastor, faith forward to possess the promise of God, trust back into the God of promise." Le Prédicateur[15]

---

[15] Journey Pastoral Coaching, Copyright © 2021

— Day 16 —

OUR FIRST AND GREATEST CARE

*"The Lord is my shepherd, I shall not want. He makes me lie down in
green pastures; He leads me beside quiet waters. He restores my soul;
He guides me in the paths of righteousness for His name's sake."*
Psalm 23:1-3

PENSÉE: SOUL HEALTH
Today and every day, Pastor, rather than focusing first on doing, let's
focus first on being.

In life and ministry, doing flows from being. If my soul is not
healthy and strong, my ministry for God cannot be life-giving. In
time, the fault lines in my soul will appear and eventually give way
to the pressures that pervade ministry life. Therefore, it is essential I
put first things first. I must make the health of my soul my first and
greatest care. I must fight for my soul as if my life – and the lives of
others – depends on it. Because, in fact, they do.

Said another way, instead of focusing first today and every day on
the ministry, let's focus first on the minister. Let's concentrate on his
Jeremiah 1.5 creation and calling. Authentic ministry for God is the
outflow of the minister's inflow from God. Like inhaling and
exhaling, healthy ministry consists of breathing out to others the life
the Holy Spirit is breathing into me – not just breathing on me, but
breathing in me in soul-transforming ways.

45

At its most fundamental level, healthy ministry is the lifestream of my personal discipleship, revealed in my character and expressed through the carrying out of my ministry calling - my being and my doing. It's growing daily in my Jeremiah 1.5 creation and calling, knowing that as I do, I naturally have life to give others. I like to say it this way: build the minister, and you build the ministry - you build them for a lifetime of healthy and effective ministry.

This has practical ramifications on our ministries, even our daily routines. First, instead of spending our first energy on accomplishing ministry tasks, we invest it in personally growing as disciples. This discipline naturally develops the muscles of our pastoral hearts and minds. We are then able to do the hands-and-feet-work of pastoring others in a healthy and effective way. Again, doing flows from being.

Second, we allow the lifestream of the Spirit to flow through us to others as we give ourselves to making disciples. Instead of spending our best energy on adding attendees to the churches we pastor, we invest our energy in making disciples of Jesus Christ. We give our lives to being and making disciples. Being and doing.

Again, as we build the minister, we naturally build the ministry. Read the Gospels. It's how Jesus developed twelve rough men into disciplined apostles and pastors who could lead the church after His ascension. If it's good enough for Jesus, it's good enough for us.

Pastor, it's time to write some new church history – page one, line one, beginning today. One of the primary plotlines of that history will be written in the investment we make in our own souls.

> *"Your own soul is your first and greatest care."* Robert Murray M'Cheyne[16]

---

[16] Taken from *Memoir and Remains of the Rev. Robert Murray M'Cheyne*, ed. Andrew A. Bonar. (Banner of Truth, Edinburgh, 1844), p. 216. Public domain.

— *Day 17* —

HEAD BOWED, HEART HUMBLE

*"He leads the humble in what is right,
and teaches the humble his way. Psalm 25.9*

PENSÉE: HUMILITY

Walk strong, Pastor, with your head bowed and your heart humble.

As itinerating missionaries, our family was ministering in a medium-sized church in a South Carolina coastal town. The pastor and church treated us like royalty. And, even better, we enjoyed a tremendous service that Sunday evening. God moved in a mighty way. After the welcome and the worship, preaching there was a delight. I took great joy in the results and the many words of blessing given us by the people as they left the sanctuary after the service concluded.

However, one man was not of their company.

When I greeted him, he grabbed my hand and pulled me up close to his bear-like body. Then, with a look of disgust, he told me, "You aren't fit to call yourself a preacher." With those words of disdain, he angrily pushed me away and left the sanctuary.

Later, I told the pastor what had happened, apologizing for any trouble I had caused him. The pastor told me, "Oh, don't worry about him. He's always mad about something. It happens all the time." With that, the pastor laughed, and I was at least assured that he was in a good place with it all. But I was not. "Not fit to call yourself a preacher." The words haunted me for days.

The following Sunday, we were back home in Indiana, preaching in a church that had recently celebrated its 50th anniversary. The service went well, and the people responded with great enthusiasm to the message. After the service, as was our custom, my wife and I stood in the church foyer by our missions display, greeting church members and answering questions about our ministry in Europe.

As the line grew shorter, I noticed an older man patiently waiting across the way. It was apparent that he wanted to be the last person to speak with us. So, as we said our thankyous and goodbyes to the person before him, this gentleman stepped forward. He took a moment to greet us and then said, "I'm a charter member of this church. This has been my home for fifty years. I've heard them all, the good preachers and the bad preachers, the well-known ones and not-so-well-known ones. But let me tell you something, you are, by far, the most powerful preacher to ever stand in our pulpit and preach the Word of God. I've never heard anyone or anything like it before."

I promise you that at that moment, I heard God speak to me, saying, "Don't believe either one of them - South Carolina or Indiana. You just do what I tell you to do and keep your heart fixed on me." I've never forgotten either man or the valuable lesson each taught me.

Walk strong, Pastor, your head bowed and your heart humble.

"He that is down needs fear no fall. He that is low, no pride; He that is humble, ever shall have God to be his Guide. John Bunyan[17]

---

[17] Taken from *The Works of John Bunyan by John Bunyan*. Public domain.

— Day 18 —

COMMUNITY

"They devoted themselves to the apostles' teaching and the fellowship, to the breaking of bread and the prayers. And awe came upon every soul, and many wonders and signs were being done through the apostles. And all who believed were together and had all things in common. And they were selling their possessions and belongings and distributing the proceeds to all, as any had need. And day by day, attending the temple together and breaking bread in their homes, they received their food with glad and generous hearts, praising God and having favor with all the people. And the Lord added to their number day by day those who were being saved."
Acts 2.42-47

PENSÉE: SHARED JOURNEY
What a novel idea: A church that emphasizes community and shared spiritual development. Why didn't someone think of this before?

Wait a minute. The description we read in Acts 2 *is* the church. Anything else is, at best, a deformed church, at worst, not the church at all. This *is* the church: the church Jesus birthed, gave life to, and grew. This is the church for which Jesus is returning. This is the New Testament church, the church for all time.

So, where are these Acts 2 churches in our time? Where are they in an increasingly individualistic church culture geared not toward Romans 12 servant-membership but John 6 consumers? Why are faith communities and shared spiritual development so hard to find when these are the church we read about in the New Testament? Why are so many churches only a schedule of Sunday services rather than the faith community we see in Acts 2?

Question: How can we uncover that church? How do we stir it to life and set it loose in all of its Spirit-fired love and life?

One way pastors can make this happen is by living in community and spiritual development ourselves. We can't give what we don't have. We can't lead others in what we do not personally possess.

But as we live in community with our pastoral peers, the lifeblood of those relationships will be evident to our people; it will flow from us into our churches, creating a shared heartbeat of life in Jesus. As we experience shared spiritual development with other pastors, the breath of those relationships will be apparent to our people; it will breathe through to them, revitalizing in us a desire for and delight in relationships. As pastors experience community and shared spiritual development, it will reproduce life in our churches.

Pastor, let's do more than call our people to be the church. Let's show the way. And a great place to start is by being a part of a community of pastors, sharing your journeys in Jesus. Not only will it help you personally experience the life of an Acts 2 faith community, but it will help you lead your church into the same life in Christ. Seeing what being a part of a faith community means to you, many in your congregation will be more than ready to join you in seeing it become your church's experience as well.

> *"In the coming years, there are going to be a lot of lonely people who didn't pay their dues when it came to building personal bonds of friendship and community. Maybe a new kind of church needs to be birthed. One that emphasizes community and spiritual development." Gordon MacDonald*[18]

---

[18] MacDonald, *Going Deep*. p.30.

— *Day 19* —

MISTAKEN IDENTITY

*"On behalf of this man I will boast, but on my own behalf I will not boast,
except of my weaknesses— though if I should wish to boast, I would not be
a fool, for I would be speaking the truth; but I refrain from it, so that no
one may think more of me than he sees in me or hears from me."*
II Corinthians 12.5-6

PENSÉE: IDENTITY

Early in his ministry life, Paul asserts his position as an Apostle.
However, by the end of his life, he claims the status of "foremost"
among sinners (I Timothy 4.15). Is Paul correct in saying he is a
sinner? Evidently. Is he right in stating he is an Apostle? Absolutely.

But the issue at hand is that of identity: Paul recognizes he is both
a sinner and an apostle. He is a man saved and serving by grace. How
can this be? How can someone be both sinner and apostle? Only
because neither is his true identity: His true identity is "child of God."

If Paul's identity is only that of a sinner, he would always wrestle
with himself for his unworthiness of person. If his identity is only that
of an apostle, he could ever wrestle with others for pride of place. But
because He is, above all, a child of God, he need only wrestle like
Jacob with God in the joyful experience of knowing God more deeply
and himself more accurately. His positions as sinner-saved-by-grace
and apostle-called-by-grace need never adversely affect him: his

identity is child of God. This is all-defining. And completely satisfying to his soul. He needs nothing more.

If Paul's foundation is not Christ and his identity is not child of God, both his sin nature and his apostleship could very well consume him with shame or pride – in either case, death by mistaken identity. But if his foundation is Christ and his identity is that of a child of God, his positions as saved sinner and sanctified apostle will consume him with overwhelming contentment and life. Shalom.

You are more than your position, Pastor. And you are more than your wrestling with sin. You are God's child, uniquely created by Him and for Him. This is who you are. You are the beloved of God.

> *"Most people go through life afraid that people will not think enough of them; Paul went through life afraid that people would think too much of him." (II Cor. 12.5-6). D.A. Carson*[19]

---

[19] Taken from *Memoirs of An Ordinary Pastor by D.A. Carson*, (Wheaton, IL: *Crossway, a publishing ministry of Good News Publishers, 2008)* p.131. *www.crossway.org*. Used by permission.

— Day 20 —

PLAN A

"Jesus came and said to them, "All authority in heaven and on earth has been given to me. Go therefore and make disciples of all nations, baptizing them in the name of the Father and of the Son and of the Holy Spirit, teaching them to observe all that I have commanded you. And behold, I am with you always, to the end of the age." Matthew 28.18-20

PENSÉE: MISSION

"Go. All nations. Make disciples. No plan B. Signed, Jesus"

The Bible is a living portrait of a missionary God, every verse of each book another brushstroke adding further depth and definition to our understanding of God's missionary heart.

When I was a missionary, I had many conversations with pastors in the US about the Great Commission. I remember one of these conversations in particular. I shared with a pastor that, in obedience to Jesus, I wanted to partner with his church, being their feet and hands to the world. He responded that God had called the church he pastored to a different mission. God may have called the missionary to reach the world, he said, but not him or his church. World missions was the missionary's call; it wasn't his.

I offered him a pair of scissors to use in cutting the Great Commission out of his Bible, warning him that he would be left with not just very little Bible but no Bible at all. Cover to cover, the basis of the Bible IS world missions: "God so loved *the world* that He gave

His only Son..." Not until all nations have heard of Jesus' first coming – and why He came - will Jesus come the second time to re-establish His kingdom, bring final judgment, and initiate the New Heavens and New Earth. Making disciples of all nations is neither a side-issue nor a "missionaries only" ministry: it is the primary ministry of the church that calls Jesus Christ its Lord.

Sadly, I didn't convince this pastor. But after all, if the Word of God couldn't convince him, why should I think I would be able to open His eyes to the clear message of the Word of God, or his heart to the loving heartbeat of the God of the Word?

Pastor, ours is a worldwide calling. So, go, preach the Gospel. Go, make disciples of all nations, beginning in the pulpit and altars of your church. Then, down the streets of your city, across your state, throughout America, and to the ends of the earth, make the ministry of Jesus your ministry until Jesus comes again.

Ours is the privilege of joining with the body of Christ around the world – and throughout history - in seeing the Great Commission of Jesus accomplished. So, preach and pastor large: all the world!

> *"Jesus came to earth the first time because of world missions: to deliver the Gospel to all. He has not yet come to earth the second time because of world missions: we have not yet delivered the Gospel to all the world. As a follower of Jesus, His mission is my mission in living every day. This day, I will live for nothing less than knowing Him more deeply that I might make Him known more widely." La Prédicateur[20]*

---

[20] Journey Pastoral Coaching, Copyright © 2021

— *Day 21* —

OUR NEED FOR PLEADERS

"I remind you to fan into flame the gift of God, which is in you through the laying on of my hands, for God gave us a spirit not of fear but of power and love and self-control." II Timothy 1.6-7

PENSÉE: IDENTITY

The weekly schedule demands. The lonely office. Or the busy one. The mail, messages, meetings, board meetings, financial reports, building demands, the low numbers, etc., all threaten to wear us down into ministry machines.

We churn out the next service schedule and sermon. We rearrange the desk. We sort and stack the mail. We do the next meeting. We respond to messages. We go over the week's tithes while looking at the bills. We deal with that building problem yet again. We have the church's master schedule waiting for us to give it our attention.

And before you know it, it's another week of more of the same, just with different names and in different degrees of intensity. Then it's ten, twenty, thirty years pastoring a church. If we can make it that long without going on autopilot and just going through the motions or burning out. Only God knows which is a greater heartbreak and tragedy – for the pastor and the members of his church.

Pastor, this is why we need "pleaders" in our lives – wise and compassionate ones who will plead with us not to press the button and put our lives on autopilot, not to go "machine" in ministry. Not cheerleaders who urge us to keep going as we're going, but those who remind us who we are, whose we are, whom we serve, and what marvelous mysteries we steward in the name of Jesus.

Let me assume the role of pleader in your life and ministry today.

God created us to be His sons and daughters, living in a vibrant and transforming relationship with Him, knowing Him ever more deeply as our Heavenly Father. "What love the Father has given us that we should be called the children of God" (I John 3.1)! You take time to focus on your to-do list every day, pastor. Maybe it's time to focus on your to-be list: I will live in who I am: a child of the Heavenly Father.

God created and called us to be pastors – not to *do* pastoring, but to *be* pastors, undershepherds of Jesus, our hearts beating in time and tune with His pastoral heart (Jeremiah 3.15).

We are His. He has created us and redeemed us – twice we belong to Him. We are His possession and the apple of His eye. We hide under the shadow of His wings (Psalm 17.8).

We serve Jesus. Not our congregations; Jesus. The service we offer our churches is ultimately service directed to Him, for He alone is our Lord. We have an audience of One. If He is pleased with us, we can be pleased with our service, pastoring tens or tens of thousands.

We are stewards of the glorious Gospel of Jesus Christ – we guard and give away the good news of His death on the Cross and resurrection from the dead to give us eternal life. This mystery is not only what we teach; it is what we treasure. For it, we live, and, if need be, would gladly die. If others do not treasure this Gospel, preferring celebrity, wealth, or leisure, that is their choice. But we are stewards of the most astonishing news in the universe: the glorious Gospel of

Jesus Christ. To this stewardship, we will be true. To this Savior, we will be joyfully faithful.

Pastor, there is no autopilot button on our flight deck, and there is no cruise control in our car. We know who we are and whose we are. We know whom we serve and what we steward in God's mysteries. This is our creation and our calling; this day and every day.

Hear the voice of this concerned pleader today, Pastor, even as he asks you to find others who will serve you as confronting, comforting, and loving pleaders in your life.

> *"It's easy for us as pastors to go on autopilot, just going through the motions of ministry, performing the roles we were trained to do without giving much thought to what we're doing. No wonder we become bored and discontent in ministry. No wonder that so many of us burn ourselves out or are such easy prey for temptations of various kinds that ruin us and end our ministries. I therefore plead with you: Watch what you're doing as a pastor. Remember who you are, whose you are, and whom you serve as a servant of Christ and steward of God's mysteries." Harold Senkbeil*[21]

---

[21] Senkbeil, p.192

— Day 22 —

BUT GOD

"O God, you are my God; earnestly I seek you;
my soul thirsts for you;
my flesh faints for you,
as in a dry and weary land where there is no water.
So I have looked upon you in the sanctuary,
beholding your power and glory.
Because your steadfast love is better than life,
my lips will praise you." Psalm 63.1-3

PENSÉE: REDEMPTION

I remember the day, even the moment when Eve (not her real name) came to our small church. She entered the sanctuary after the worship service had started, taking a seat in the last row on the center aisle. I was standing in the pulpit at the time. When she entered, I sensed death had entered the room. That sense came not only from my spirit but from the deathly pall on her face.

The service continued as usual. I preached the message God had laid on my heart, a message on the power of God to save, heal, and deliver. I closed the service with an unusual altar call. I invited everyone in the sanctuary to gather together around the altars. These were the early days of our ministry at this church, a church on life-support at the time. The church was small, meaning everyone could squeeze together in a large circle around the altar area.

The entire church came forward - even Eve. Imagine my surprise when she did not exit the sanctuary but came on her own to the altars. To my great joy, she stood with everyone else as I encouraged everyone to bring their needs, whatever they were facing, themselves, to God, believing He was able and willing to meet them there with His love and power.

People began to pray, holding each other's hands, lifting their voices to God. I could sense faith rising. My eyes fell on Eve, and to my amazement, she had raised her hands along with the two people on either side of her. Tears were streaming down her face. Not knowing her or her situation, I did not know what God was doing in her heart. At the close of our service, I learned her remarkable story.

Eve came to our church that morning facing an impossible situation. She was being threatened and harassed by a husband she had divorced for physical abuse. She would move, he would track her down, and the threats would begin again. Not even injunctions could stop him. She was literally in fear of her life to the point that she had suffered emotional breakdown after emotional breakdown, spending almost all she had on treatment. She had lived with her brother for months until he and his family could no longer deal with her deep trauma. Finally, Eve's brother told her he was sorry, but he had done all he could to help her. She would have to leave his home. There was a church a few streets away, he told her. Maybe the people there could help her. He would take her there in time for the worship service the next morning.

With this last bridge burned and no hope for the future. Eve made her decision. She packed her few things. She emptied her purse of everything but one possession: a handgun. Suitcase and purse in hand, she sat silently in the car as her brother drove her to our church. Arriving, they said their goodbyes, and he dropped her off. She entered the building where she set her case in the vestibule before entering the sanctuary to make her peace with God. When service was over, she would then walk out into the woods behind our property, where she would take her life.

But God met her in a powerful way that morning. She came to the altars to make her peace and die, but God met her at the altar to give her peace so that she might live. It was a breaking of death and a birthing of life I will never forget. It was evident for all to see: death had given way to life!

And live she did. We helped her as we could, and she was back in church the following week where God did the second half of an incredible work in her life – a moment that was a turning point of faith in our church, a prophetic action of the miracle God was working in her life and in our faith community.

Eve was a wonderful part of our church for the next too-few years before moving to another state. If you had been in our church on her last Sunday with us and I had shown you a picture of Eve on her first day with us, you would never have believed it was the same woman. Darkness and death had given way to beauty and life.

After she left, Eve called and checked in from time to time, telling us all God was doing in her life and thanking us for all our part in her redemption story. What she never really understood was how much she and her story meant to us.

But God, Pastor. But, God.

"Christianity is a power religion. Christ has the power to re-create men from the inside out, as every man who has ever met Him knows." Peter Marshall[22]

---

[22] Taken from *The Light and the Glory* by Peter Marshall. (Grand Rapids: Fleming H. Revell, 1980). p.375. Used by permission.

— *Day 23* —

SOUND MINISTRY

"I charge you in the presence of God and of Christ Jesus, who is to judge the living and the dead, and by his appearing and his kingdom: preach the word; be ready in season and out of season; reprove, rebuke, and exhort, with complete patience and teaching. For the time is coming when people will not endure sound teaching, but having itching ears they will accumulate for themselves teachers to suit their own passions, and will turn away from listening to the truth and wander off into myths. As for you, always be sober-minded, endure suffering, do the work of an evangelist, fulfill your ministry." II Timothy 4.1-5

PENSÉE: THE FAITH

Christian doctrine is under attack.

The words of Paul to Timothy are being proven true in our day: many in the church of Jesus Christ cannot endure sound doctrine. Entertaining stories, yes. Strong doctrine, no.

Many in the Church today are teaching that doctrine is less rather than more important. "Yes," they say, "doctrine has its place, but it's getting in the way of the work of the Church." These assert that focusing on doctrine has weakened the Church and its witness. Interesting. So, what then is this black leather book, and why is it cluttering up my pastoral desk and pulpit? More to the point, why has the Church so allowed it to clutter its history?

So-called experts tell us we need to rethink or "evolve" in our thinking when it comes to what have been the cardinal doctrines of

63

the church for 21 centuries, the message of the people of God since
our beginning. Even many of America's "must hear" preachers
advocate for a lesser-rather-than-greater emphasis on doctrine during
this time of relativism. As if Paul didn't have to deal with relativism,
multi-culturalism, and pluralism in his time. What was he thinking,
writing epistles of strong doctrine when the Roman Empire offered a
full range of self-service religions and philosophies?

That calls for the disdain and dismissal of doctrine would come
from American culture is not surprising – the world is offended by
even the idea of absolute truth. But the Church itself seems to be
nodding off in agreement. That these calls for the reduction and
rejection of doctrine would come from within the Church is
absolutely stunning. In fact, for the Church to diminish the vital
importance of doctrine is nothing short of suicidal. We owe our very
existence to doctrine – without it, we are not the church. And we have
no Gospel to proclaim:

> "No one can say 'Jesus is Lord' (1 Cor. 12:3; Rom. 10:9) without
> speaking in a deeply doctrinal way, because this simple statement
> rests on profound biblical truths. It assumes that Christ is the
> eternal second member of the Trinity, who became uniquely God
> incarnate, was set forth as our substitutionary atonement, was
> raised from the dead having conquered all evil, and is now
> reigning sovereignly over all reality" (Ephesians 1:20–22). Tim
> Challies[23]

Recent polls reveal these attacks on doctrine have been
frighteningly successful: large numbers of Americans reject cardinal

---

[23] Challies, Tim. "What Is Doctrine and Why Is It Important?" *Challies.com*. Tim
Challies, 2002-2021, 25 September 2017,
https://www.challies.com/sponsored/what-is-doctrine-and-why-is-it-important/.
Used by permission.

Christian doctrines. Many are ravenously taking bite after bite of the apple of Eden, amening each other, "Has God really said?" (Gen. 3.1) Not only do vast numbers of Americans now reject Christian doctrine, but studies of the Evangelical Church are not at all encouraging. Increasing numbers of Evangelicals reject cardinal Christian doctrine as well. If these multiple studies are accurate, our churches are filled with people who do not know Jesus Christ. Seated in the presence of God, they are far from Him. Why? For lack of knowledge – the absence of doctrine – the "people of God" are perishing (Hosea 4.6).

Dorothy Sayers was a 20th-century writer and philosopher. She was a close friend of J.R.R Tolkien and C.S. Lewis, and a "satellite" member of The Inklings, the renowned circle of thinkers and writers. Writing seventy years ago in an England that went the way of apostasy ahead of us, Sayers had this prophetic word for England in her time and America in ours:

"Christianity, of late years, has been having what is known as a bad press. We are constantly assured that the churches are empty because preachers insist too much upon doctrine—dull dogma as people call it. The fact is the precise opposite. It is the neglect of dogma that makes for dullness. The Christian faith is the most exciting drama that ever staggered the imagination of man—and the dogma is the drama." Dorothy L. Sayers[24]

"Dogma – doctrine – IS the drama."

Pastor, preach and teach the Word. Do not yield to the pressures of the culture around your church or the culture within your church. As a soldier of Jesus Christ, preach the Word. As a faithful

---

[24] Sayers, Dorothy. *Letters to a Diminished Church.* (Nashville: Thomas Nelson, 2004), p.1. Used by permission.

undershepherd of Jesus Christ, teach the Word. As one who speaks for God, preach the Word to a lost and dying world.

Preach the Word.

> *(Unless the church embraces theology and teaches doctrine) "Christianity will remain simply a cultural convenience that will be discarded every time its teaching threatens our way of life. It will be powerless to yield the meaning that we need, powerless to preserve us in the way of God as we seek." David F. Wells[25]*

---

[25] Taken from *No Place For Truth* by David F. Wells. (Grand Rapids: Wm. B. Eerdmans, 1993), p.254. Used by permission.

— Day 24 —

UNDERSHEPHERDS

"I thank him who has given me strength, Christ Jesus our Lord, because he judged me faithful, appointing me to his service." I Timothy 1.12

PENSÉE: SERVANTHOOD

During one of our family's missionary itineration cycles, a dog breeder blessed us with a beautiful six-week-old Shetland Sheep Dog we named Cinnamon. Little did I know how deeply into my heart she would dive and how closely we would share life.

She could read my mind, and yes, there were times when she spoke her mind to me. But it was always as part of a loving partnership in which she lived and breathed only to please me and share my life. If our family went to the backyard, Cinnamon followed. If my daughters didn't obey me quickly enough to suit her, Cinnamon would circle and corral them in ever tighter rings until they "got in line." If I wanted to be quiet in my chair, she lay by my side. If it was time to climb in the van for yet another of our many ministry trips, she eagerly jumped in and contentedly found her place. She was more than a dog to me; she was family. She was a part of my heart.

Cinnamon was happy to be a part, always trusting even when it meant challenging tasks like going to the veterinarian. If I told her to follow me, she did just that, and with joy at sharing the journey. She never raced ahead or fell behind but always walked by my side unless

I released her to run or commanded her to stay. Hers was the heart of a ready servant. And never did she fail to express her unbounded joy at my presence. A month or a day apart from each other was the same to her: she always greeted me as if I was the most important person in the world. Perhaps in her world, I was.

Pastor, we can take a lesson from the four-legged shepherds that serve their human masters so faithfully. Like them, we don't always see the big picture of life or our service – but the Great Good Shepherd does. We aren't the Mastermind, pulling the levers to make the church effective in its mission or move people to live in the full blessing of God – but the Great Good Shepherd is. We aren't even the source of our own joy. He is. One thought of Him and His great love for us is all we need to set our hearts racing: He is ours, and we are His! And together with the Great Good Shepherd, we are privileged to do life and ministry as undershepherds with Him.

May we be faithful servants, ever captivated by His love!

> *"What enthralls me about the picture of a dog in the service of his master are three things. First, the dog can't possibly know or even begin to grasp the whole of the shepherd's intent. Second, he's not self-assertive, but only serves as an extension of the shepherd's heart and directive will. He is an agent of another mind, at the willing and eager disposal of the shepherd, doing his bidding and finding great delight in the process. He can afford to take his time, confident and assertive but never aggressive. Finally, despite the frustrations caused by the sheep, the dog's tail is always wagging, because he is completely captivated by his love for the shepherd." Harold Senkbeil*[26]

---

[26] Senkbeil, p.123.

— Day 25 —

DEAD RELIGION

"Now about eight days after these sayings he took with him Peter and John and James and went up on the mountain to pray. And as he was praying, the appearance of his face was altered, and his clothing became dazzling white. And behold, two men were talking with him, Moses and Elijah, who appeared in glory and spoke of his departure, which he was about to accomplish at Jerusalem. Now Peter and those who were with him were heavy with sleep, but when they became fully awake they saw his glory."
Luke 9.28-32

PENSÉE: THE FAITH

Pastor, if it's dead religious services you want, the funeral home is down the street and around the corner.

But we, the Church of Jesus Christ, do not gather on Sunday to bury the dead. We come to meet with our God and our Maker. We gather together to gaze upon His beauty, to worship and celebrate Him who is our Creator and Redeemer. We come to enter His holy presence, to know His love and power. We gather to be transformed by the Living God that we might then return, empowered, to our places of service in the world.

As an itinerating missionary, I preached in hundreds of church services. Most of them were celebrations of a living Savior. Believers entered the gates of God with thanksgiving in their hearts, His courts with praise (Psalm 100.4)! Churches like these ministered far more to me than I ever ministered to them. But, sadly, there were those churches where I found myself looking for a coffin: the "worship" was so lifeless it could only mean someone had died.

How can this be? Dead worship in the presence of a living God? Faith funerals during the hour of worship? God forbid! As the angel said, "He is not here (in this or any tomb). He is risen!" And because He is risen, He is alive and on the move in our midst, ready to renew us and work wonders among us if we will allow Him to do so.

Let others gather in their spiritual funeral homes on Sunday. But as for us, we choose to make our way to God's Upper Room, where Jesus waits to baptize us in His power and love again and again -every time we meet in His name. We choose to make of our church a holy Upper Room where men and women know that they know that their God is in the house. He was here before we arrived, waiting for us, anticipating this time and all that He will do – if only we allow Him. We choose to make our church an Upper Room where week by week (why not day by day), God shakes the house with His person and power, saving, healing, and setting people free.

We choose to worship the living Lord! We choose to come to a living Jesus in all of His glory!

> *"The greatest problem in the world today is dead religion. Dead religion breeds death and comfortable co-habitation with evil, an easy acceptance of compromise. Dead religion aids and abets the spirit of death that is consuming this world and people for whom Jesus died." La Prédicateur*[27]

---

[27] Journey Pastoral Coaching, Copyright © 2021

— Day 26 —

HIM

"In Him, we live, move and have our being." Acts 17.28

PENSÉE: PREACHING

As pastor-preachers, we have one life-consuming passion: Jesus Christ. He is our life. Indeed, "In Him, we live, move and have our being" (Acts 17.28).

Though not usually the first New Testament book we look to in the study of Christology, Philippians contains four precious "Jesus-promises" from God to us, four eternal treasures that are ours as we make Jesus the object of our own supreme love and confidence...

He is the *purpose* of our life: "For to me to live is Christ, and to die is gain." (1.21)

He is the *pattern* of our life: "Let this mind be in you that was in Christ Jesus." (2.5)

He is our *prize* in life: "I press on toward the goal for the prize of the upward call of God in Christ Jesus" (3.21).

He is the *power* of our life: "I can do all things through Him who strengthens me" (4.13)

The more deeply we possess these truths, the more deeply they possess us, the more they come alive in our daily living. They become heartbeats in our souls. We cease preaching about Christ and begin preaching Him. In all of His majesty, we present the glorious Christ.

71

He is no longer a sermon subject; He is our very life: our purpose, our pattern, our prize, and our power. We preach Him as an act of worship, loving Him with all of our heart, soul, mind, and strength.

Yes, it is essential we preach the doctrines of the Word of God (II Timothy 4.1-3); we teach disciples to "observe all that (Jesus) has commanded you" (Matthew 28.20). But preaching is not a Jesus Christ *or* doctrine dilemma: these two are the same in essence and purpose. In preaching and teaching His doctrines, we not only show "The Way" of Jesus, but we present the living Christ Himself. Through our preaching, we believe He will stand in the very midst of His people in all of His saving power and glory. Through our presentation of the King of Kings in His beauty and wonder, men and women will see Him as the Apostle John saw Him on the Island of Patmos: majestic, radiant, and full of grace.

Not because we love preaching, but because we love Him, every sermon is an opportunity to present the object of our love to everyone under the sound of our voice. Our purpose in preaching is that He may become the life-consuming object of their love as well, that they, too, will say in their heart of hearts, "In Him, I live and move and have my being" (Acts 17.28).

> *"Preaching Christ does not mean merely to preach his doctrines, but to preach him as the object of supreme love and confidence." Charles Hodge.*[28]

---

[28] Taken from *A Commentary on the Epistle to the Ephesians* by Charles Hodge. Public domain.

— Day 27 —

DARK NIGHT OF THE SOUL

"How long, O Lord? Will you forget me forever?
How long will you hide your face from me?
How long must I take counsel in my soul
and have sorrow in my heart all the day?
How long shall my enemy be exalted over me?
Consider and answer me, O Lord my God;
light up my eyes, lest I sleep the sleep of death,
lest my enemy say, "I have prevailed over him,"
lest my foes rejoice because I am shaken.
But I have trusted in your steadfast love;
my heart shall rejoice in your salvation.
I will sing to the Lord,
because he has dealt bountifully with me."
Psalm 13.1-6

PENSÉE: DEPTH
What a terrible and beautiful thought that God would seem to remove
His presence from our lives so He might dwell in us more deeply. It's
an experience known to all devoted followers of Jesus and especially
to faithful shepherds of God's people.

How we long to know the depths of God's nature and presence.
How we yearn to know Him in all of His grace, love, and power. Yet,
how little we understand the way that leads us there. Given a choice,
we would dance and sing our way into the Holy of Holies, not
understanding the way to truly know Him must, at some point, take

73

us to a cross and our own heart cry, "Lord, why have you forgotten me?"

But God often makes His presence known to us by His absence. As we wonder at His seeming separation, we seek Him, willing to break through the floors of our lives to find Him, ready even to be broken ourselves.

Breaking and being broken. Wrestling. Like Jacob with the angel, we cry out, "I will not let you go until you bless me." Like the angel wrestling with Jacob, "I will not let go of you until I transform you." Often in breaking and being broken.

But it is in wrestling with God intensely that we come to know Him deeply. It is in allowing God to wrestle with us, using the tool of silence and seeming separation, that we are transformed and formed into vessels into which He can pour Himself.

It is in seeking Him intensely, even desperately, that we find a depth of His presence we have never known or even imagined before. No longer is His promise to be present with us only print-on-page doctrine, but breath and blood reality: "He *is* my Emmanuel; He *is* God with me."

God's answer to our cross and cry is as sure and trustworthy as Himself. There may be a "crucified-with-Christ" Friday (Galatians 2.20) and even a Saturday of silence and wonder after our cross. But Sunday is coming and with it the Living One, He who is our Resurrection and Life, the very life for which we have yearned.

On that day, let our celebrations in the presence of God be full and free. Let our joy be unbounded. But even now, as we wonder at His seeming absence, let us trust in His steadfast love. Let us rejoice in His salvation, knowing He always deals bountifully with us.

Yes, Pastor, to lead us more deeply into Himself, God may give us the gift of a dark night of the soul. But weeping only endures for a night. There is joy, ever deeper joy, in the morning.

"The 'dark night of the soul' (St. John of the Cross) is that time when people lose the joy they once experienced in their spiritual disciplines and faith practices. John taught that this happens because God wants to purify their souls and move them to deeper faith. In the beginning of faith, God will move gently a person's life, like a mother with an infant, seeking to nurture and care for the child. As time proceeds, however, there comes a time for the child to grow into adulthood, and God invites them to grow through the experiences of the dark night of the soul. The perceived darkness is that time when God appears to withdraw from the individual. It is often a time of intense difficulty as a person of faith undergoes the loss of the sense of God's active presence. The reward is purification of the soul that furthers faith development." Keith R. Anderson and Randy D. Reece[29]

---

[29] Taken from *Spiritual Mentoring* by Keith R. Anderson and Randy D. Reece. (Downers Grove: InterVarsity Press, 1999). p.114. Used by permission.

— Day 28 —

GRACE & GRATITUDE

"And let the peace of Christ rule in your hearts, to which indeed you were called in one body. And be thankful. Let the word of Christ dwell in you richly, teaching and admonishing one another in all wisdom, singing psalms and hymns and spiritual songs, with thankfulness in your hearts to God. And whatever you do, in word or deed, do everything in the name of the Lord Jesus, giving thanks to God the Father through him."
Colossians 3.15-17

PENSÉE: GRACE
Three times in three sentences, the Apostle Paul invites the people of God to live a full life of grace. His prescription for knowing and living in God's grace is gratitude, a thankful heart:

- v.15: "And be thankful;"
- v.16: "With thankfulness in your hearts to God;"
- v.17: "Whatever you do... giving thanks to God the Father through him."

A thankful heart is essential in pastoral ministry. It pumps the blood of God's grace through our system. Without a heart of gratitude, we can't survive the long journey of shepherding the sheep of God's pasture. But with a heart of gratitude, we thrive.

I know my pastoral heart is weak when the pulse of my personal gratitude is faint. The absence of verbal thanks to God and others is a heart stress test, telling me there is a problem that must be addressed. I can address it through the drugs of diversions (TV, sports, hobbies, etc.), or I can give my heart what it needs: gratitude. Expressing gratitude from my heart to God and others releases grace in my being, and with it, health to my soul.

Yes, some churches make it more challenging to have a thankful heart. But if a church has more influence than the God of grace on my attitude of gratitude, maybe it's time for some heart surgery. Our God and His grace are greater than any circumstance. Or church.

Do yourself a favor and ask friends to assist you in performing a stress test on your heart: ask them about your language. Is it filled with complaint or thanksgiving, criticism or praise? Yes, lament is a part of godly, holy pastoral language, but only as it is sandwiched between the bread of thanks. Try it, praise-wrapped lament not only tastes better than bare complaints, but it satisfies our hunger for meaning and supplies great strength to continue on. It sets our heartache and heart in the hands of our Lord.

Why merely survive on a diet of complaints or a life empty of thanks? Be a scout for grace! Look for God's grace everywhere every day. And every time you see it, respond to God from a grateful heart, "Thank you, my Father."

> *"Gratitude bestows reverence, allowing us to encounter everyday epiphanies, those transcendent moments of awe that change forever how we experience life and the world." John Milton*[30]

---

[30] John Milton, public domain.

— Day 29 —

TRIAL BY FIRE

*"Count it all joy, my brothers, when you meet trials of various kinds, for
you know that the testing of your faith produces steadfastness. And let
steadfastness have its full effect, that you may be perfect and complete,
lacking in nothing." James 1.2-4*

PENSÉE: TRIALS

A challenging thought today, Pastor, but an essential one for
surviving and thriving in the life to which God has called us.

Ours is not a country club life. It is an "in the trenches" one that
knows hard work, testing, and even tribulations that would seem to
push us beyond our ability to endure. Often, our mirrors and our
friends-of-Job ask us, "Where is your God in these things? Has He
forgotten you? Is He unfaithful to Himself and you?"

No, we answer, quite the opposite; he is ever faithful in these
things. He remains "Emmanuel," God with us. The God who suffered
to deliver salvation to us permits us to enter into His sufferings for
our own sake, and that we "may be able to comfort those who are in
any affliction, with the comfort with which we ourselves are
comforted by God" (II Corinthians1.4). Because we know suffering,
we can compassionately serve God's people as true shepherds.

God allows us to experience trials and even pain so we can know
the Savior more deeply. In Philippians 3.10, Paul opens his prayer

journal to us, "That I may know him, and the power of his resurrection and share in the fellowship of his sufferings."

In I Peter 2.21, Peter reminds believers, "For to this you have been called, because Christ also suffered for you, leaving you an example, so that you might follow in his steps."

And again, "Therefore let those who suffer according to God's will entrust their souls to a faithful Creator while doing good" (I Peter 4.19).

Suffering for Christ leads disciples to trust their souls even more deeply to a faithful Creator.

We know Jesus more meaningfully, and even more powerfully, in this life because we have known pain, and the Savior has met us there. Isn't this worth the price of suffering for His name's sake?

Finally, God permits us to experience just a small measure of His sufferings that we might know an even greater and eternal glory with Him. Presaging what his fellow apostle, Peter, will later write, Paul encourages us with these words:

> "For this light momentary affliction is preparing for us an eternal weight of glory beyond all comparison, as we look not to the things that are seen but to the things that are unseen. For the things that are seen are transient, but the things that are unseen are eternal." (II Corinthians 4.17-18).

In the life to come, Jesus will open more of His glory to us because we have known suffering in this life as we have ministered in His name.

Press on, Pastor! A greater weight of glory awaits us in the life to come. And even now, as we labor for Him, a greater sense of His presence and a more Jesus-filled ministry will be ours.

"Good men are promised tribulation in this world, and ministers may expect a larger share than others, that they may learn sympathy with the Lord's suffering people, and so may be fitting shepherds of an ailing flock." C.H. Spurgeon[31]

[31] Taken from *Lectures to My Students* C.H. Spurgeon. (Grand Rapids: Zondervan, 1977) p.155. Used by permission.

— *Day 30* —

GOD OF WONDERS

"When the disciples heard this, they were greatly astonished, saying, "Who then can be saved?" But Jesus looked at them and said, "With man this is impossible, but with God all things are possible." Matthew 19.25-26

PENSÉE: POWER

It was on this day, over three decades ago, that our first daughter was born. Miracle of miracles!

I remember driving my wife down State Boulevard in Fort Wayne, Indiana, in the pre-dawn hours for the induced delivery. Our little girl would enter the world weighing more than ten pounds, the extra emphasis of God on a birth that should never have happened.

You see, doctors had told us we would never be able to have children. Impossible. Not going to happen. Their counsel was to know the joy of parenthood by adopting. After prayer, we made the decision to follow the doctors' counsel. We called our denominational adoption agency to ask about the process and request literature. That evening, we called our parents to tell them what the doctors had told us and what we had decided to do. They shared our sorrow but were glad to hear of our decision to pursue adoption. Both sets of parents assured us they were ready to do whatever they could to help. After each conversation, we hung up the phone, thankful for our parents and encouraged by their support, but feeling as if we had just attended a funeral, the funeral of our own child, a child we had never met.

About forty days later, we had to call our parents again and tell them we had been wrong: we were expecting our first child. The reality that excellent doctors had previously told us we would have to accept, God had superseded with a higher reality we accepted with delight beyond all description. Seven years of waiting, hoping, and praying. Two months of sorrow, tears, and pain. It was all baptized in joy and gratitude to God for His blessing.

All of this was in our hearts and minds as we drove to the hospital that October 27th morning. To the hum of the car engine, we remembered and rehearsed the history of the miracle God had already performed and were about to see delivered. It was a miracle God was to repeat three years later with the birth of our second beautiful daughter.

As Jesus said, a situation may be impossible for people, but all things are possible with God. He is the Creator God, the God who can speak to nothing and from it create a universe of galaxies, stars, planets, lands, plants, and animals. Even little ones who will one day call out to Him in love and trust, "Heavenly Father."

Pastor, this is your all-things-are-possible day and life. Dare to bring your impossibilities to God, believing He is still in the business of making them come true.

"We have a God who delights in impossibilities." Billy Sunday[32]

---

[32] Billy Sunday, public domain.

— *Day 31* —

PASTOR-FOR-LIFE

"So I exhort the elders among you, as a fellow elder and a witness of the sufferings of Christ, as well as a partaker in the glory that is going to be revealed: shepherd the flock of God that is among you, exercising oversight, not under compulsion, but willingly, as God would have you; not for shameful gain, but eagerly; not domineering over those in your charge, but being examples to the flock. 1 Peter 5.1-3

PENSÉE: PRIVILEGE
What a privilege it is to be shepherds of the flock of God! It is a ministry role that leads us into a special relationship with God and with His people. As His undershepherd, we come to know and depend on Him as we never dreamed possible. As a pastor to His church, we come to know and delight in His people as we never imagined.

To be a pastor is to be *passionate for God*. It is to respond to the call of God - the God who called us not just once years ago, but every day of our life, the call to come away with Him and be with Him.

To be a pastor is to be *compassionate with God's people,* walking with them as a loving shepherd. Yes, there are the rare obstinate sheep in God's pasture, but by and large, what a joy it is to walk with the people of God, to share their lives and journeys in Jesus. What a joy and privilege it is to hear someone say, "Pastor,…"

Pastor, you belong to God. You are His - a pastor for life. This is not a job. It is a calling, and even more, it is who you are. Whatever your position, you are a pastor in creation and call. God has formed you and summoned you to shepherd His people. Like Jesus in John 10, you call them by name and speak to them as their shepherd. You anoint their wounds and help them find healing. You lead and feed them. You help them find rest for their souls in this often hard world.

I've pastored many people over the years. I'm still in touch with a good number of them. And from time to time (but not often enough), I am blessed to see them face-to-face. What joy fills my heart every time we can spend even a few minutes together.

A few years ago, I preached for a friend "back home in Indiana." Imagine my surprise and delight when about a dozen people from a church I once pastored were in attendance. They had driven in from a neighboring city to see me. I can't express how it warmed my heart to see them and "be their pastor" again for just a little while. And then greeting them after service as they embraced me again as their pastor. Not past tense. But present and precious tense.

This brings me to a privilege we don't recognize enough: how the people we pastor minister to us.

My wife and I had been through so much with the group of people who came that day. We had worked together to save and restore a broken church. We had worshipped God together through the darkest of times and the most glorious of seasons. We had laughed and cried together. They were there for the births of our daughters. They were there to comfort us in our times of loss. They were there with special blessings on Pastor Appreciation Day and Christmas, or for no reason at all but love. Time and again, they had anointed our lives with oil and called us by name, "Pastor."

To be a pastor is to be passionate for God. And it is to be compassionate with God's people, walking with them as a loving shepherd, *sharing life's journey together*.

What a privilege to hear people we love say to us, "Pastor."

"I have always loved the sound of the word (pastor). From an early age, the word called to mind a person who is passionate for God and compassionate with people....Today still, when people ask me what I want to be called, I always say, "Pastor."
Eugene Peterson[33]

---

[33] Taken from *The Contemplative Pastor* by Eugene Peterson. (Grand Rapids: Wm. B. Eerdmans, 1989), p.15. Used by permission.

— Day 32 —

DEATH BY ISOLATION

Look to the right and see:
there is none who takes notice of me;
no refuge remains to me;
no one cares for my soul. Psalm 142.3

PENSÉE: RELATIONSHIPS

I'll say it again: the number one killer of ministers is isolation. Like a lover, it woos us. Like a jealous lover, it demands we separate ourselves from all potential rivals. There, in the aroma of its warm and shadowy embrace, it convinces us that not only do we not need others, but we are better off without them.

And the proof that we are better off without others? The fact that they don't call or come looking for us. Yes, we know they have offered themselves one hundred and one times, but the fact that they didn't come one hundred and two times reveals their true colors. Yes, we know that we did not respond when they reached out to us one hundred and one times, but if they really cared, they would have persevered. They would have reached out in another way.

And so, alone in the suffocating embrace of our lover called isolation, we sit in our happy misery, convinced that we are better off without people: no people, no pain; no people, no one rocking our little boat of self and self-pity. Feeling completely justified in rejecting others' attempts to reach us, the young minister pulls the plug on his ministry, and the older minister puts it in cruise and just rides it out to the horizon of retirement.

Isolation wins. But who loses?

Who loses? The people who called you "Pastor" and the peers who would like to call you friend – they all lose.

The people in your neighborhood who don't know Jesus, and those around the world who have yet to hear – they lose, too.

Your mate and children lose as they wonder, "Who is this person we no longer recognize? This person we so deeply need?"

Who loses? How about God, the One who called you? The Heavenly Father, the One who created you for so much more than death by isolation?

Who loses? At the end of the day, you lose. For you have squandered some of God's most precious gifts in life: your creation and your calling. And you have missed the relationships we all need to survive and thrive. You lose most of all because you have lost yourself. And before God, that is the greatest loss of all.

It's time to kill the killer, Pastor. Declare death to isolation.

Isolation kills younger ministers by convincing them to quit the ministry. Isolation kills older ministers by convincing them to quit ministering in the ministry. The younger terminates his ministry life while the older sets his life on cruise and rides it out to retirement. Le Prédicateur[34]

---

[34] Journey Pastoral Coaching, Copyright © 2021

— Day 33 —

UNDERSHEPHERDS OF JESUS

"And I will give you shepherds after my own heart, who will feed you with knowledge and understanding." Jeremiah 3.15

PENSÉE: HUMILITY

How easily we pastors can be impressed with ourselves. And how willingly. "People come to me because I have the answers. I meet their needs. I am God's servant. All of this tells me how much people need me."

Me.

How easily my ego is stoked and stroked. And, without humility, how easily my ego can be crushed when I realize the truth: people need me, but only because they need Jesus. I am just the undershepherd He has sent in His stead.

In the Old and New Testaments, God encourages us with the news that He has given pastors to His people, undershepherds of the Great Good Shepherd. Ephesians 4 says the office or role of pastor is a gift to the church, universal and local. God then selects individuals to serve local churches as His undershepherds. Knowing none of us are sufficient for the task, the Great Good Shepherd equips us for the work of pastoring His people. It is not by our abilities or giftings alone that we shepherd His people. It is by His life-giving breath and anointing as we daily answer His call to pastor His people. Our abilities and giftings are involved, but they only carry life as they are infused with the life of the Spirit. But filled with His breath and under His pastoral anointing, we are well able to pastor His people as His humble but confident undershepherds.

No, Christ's sheep don't need us because of us, but they do need us. Consider Matthew 9.36:

"But when Jesus saw the multitudes, He was moved with compassion for them, because they were weary and scattered, like sheep having no shepherd."

"Like sheep having no shepherd."

Without a shepherd, God's people become weary and scatter, helpless in the world before the enemies of their soul. But in His great compassion, Jesus has given a great gift to the church: the office of pastor. A shepherd who watches over their souls (Hebrews 13.17).

And in His great wisdom, Jesus has provided another precious gift to the church: His shepherd's anointing. A shepherd's anointing is unlike any other in the church, for it is the spark of the Spirit that enables pastors, human vessels, to see people through the Good Shepherd's eyes, to have compassion on them with the Good Shepherd's heart, and to strengthen them with the Good Shepherd's hand. A shepherd's anointing enables human vessels to shepherd God's people as the eyes, heart, and hands of Jesus extended.

Thank God! We are undershepherds of the Great Good Shepherd.

"Christ's sheep need you, but only because they need Jesus."
Harold Senkbeil[35]

---

[35] Senkbeil, p.277.

— Day 34 —

GOD YEARNS

*"See what kind of love the Father has given to us, that we should be called
children of God; and so we are. The reason why the world does not know
us is that it did not know him. Beloved, we are God's children now, and
what we will be has not yet appeared; but we know that when he appears
we shall be like him, because we shall see him as he is." I John 3.1-2*

PENSÉE: THE LOVE OF GOD
I have a confession to make: I have a wife. And a girlfriend. And a
bride. It's true. And all three are the same person: the beautiful
woman with whom I shared "I do's" over forty years ago.

The girlfriend of her causes me to joyfully strive to win her heart
again each day. What can I do to make her mine?

The bride of her makes me long to possess her now that she has
said yes and entered in the covenant of marriage with me.

The woman of her makes my heart skip a beat, and I find myself
wanting to know more of the wonder-filled person she is – her beauty,
strength, wisdom, and love.

The wife in her makes me yearn to share every heartbeat and
breath of a more than forty-year deep and fresh love in which we are
one flesh and daily experiencing more and more of what that means.
And it is all fueled by her yearning for me. Her love for me stirs up a
longing in me to respond to her and her love.

Why is it this way?

First, the Trinity God. In His three-part relationship within Himself, God is perfect love. He wants us to know that love by entering into relationship with Him. Rather than only telling us He loves us, He demonstrates this love in sending His Son to die on the Cross to pay for our sins. Rather than only talk about this love, He reveals this love by sending His Spirit to bear witness with us that we are the children of God and to guide us in The Way that leads ever more deeply into life.

Second, God reveals to us the gift of covenant love in a way we can readily understand. He makes His love tangible by giving us someone like us, yet different from us - a husband or wife - with whom we can experience a measure of His love. Someone who reflects God's image as we do, but in a different and captivating way. God wants us to know and enjoy His gift of ultimate human love for its own sake – just as He gave Adam and Eve to one another. But even more, He gives us the present of covenant marriage love so we will understand His love.

Now let's pull back the curtain on my relationship with my wife so we might understand a great mystery. As I pursue my girlfriend, I see that she has been pursuing me all along! Possessing my bride, I realize she is possessing me! My heart skipping a beat at her love for me, I grasp that her heart skips a beat over me! My heart yearning to share every heartbeat and breath with her, I realize that her heart has long been yearning to share every heartbeat and breath with me.

And here's the true wonder: As I consider the love I share with my wife, I realize she is a living parable of the loving God who has been pursuing me, possessing me, skipping a beat over me, and yearning to share every heartbeat and breath with me.

Or do I? Do I realize God's yearning for me?

Do you, Pastor? You're occupied telling people of God's love for them, working to draw them together in that love, putting in overtime to lead them into His love, but are you as occupied with God's yearning for you? Are you daily overwhelmed by His love for you? Every child of God needs to realize this truth, but it is vital for a pastor. You and I "handle" His love every day, so much so it can become fact but not truth, reality but not real, a lesson but not life. Pastor, today – now – take a moment, an hour, or an entire day, and remember, maybe even realize for the first time God's yearning for YOU and His skipping heartbeat over YOU.

> *"God's yearning for us stirs up our longing in response. God's initiating presence may be ever so subtle – an inward tug of desire, a more than coincidence meeting of words and events, a glimpse of the beyond in a storm or in a flower – but it is enough to make the heart skip a beat and to make us want to know more." Howard Macy*[36]

---

[36] Taken from *Rhythms of the Inner Life* by Howard Macy. (Old Tappan: Fleming H. Revell, 1988), p.21. Used by permission.

— Day 35 —

TRUTH ON FIRE

"My message and my preaching were not in persuasive words of wisdom, but in demonstration of the Spirit and of power, so that your faith would not rest on the wisdom of men, but on the power of God.
I Corinthians 2.4-5

PENSÉE: THE WORD OF GOD
When was the last time you left the sanctuary unable to speak because God had just powerfully and definitively spoken - there was nothing left for anyone to say? When was the last time you were shaken to the depths of your soul by the preaching of God's Word – you were convicted of sin, convinced of His love, challenged to take up your cross, confident to carry the Gospel to nations? When was the last time you trembled at the proclamation of the Word of God - the Truth echoed in power with signs following, and lives were changed?

We have oceans of messages from preachers, words stamped "prophetic," but is there no word from the Lord? We have a plethora of Sunday therapy sessions and how-to seminars, but is there no word from the Creator? We have a traffic jam of pulpit celebrity pageants framed for flat screen programming, but is there no word from the Redeemer? We have an abundance of talkers' thoughts about God, but is there no word from the Logos – a life-giving, soul-saving, holiness-inducing, relationship-mending, world-transforming word from the Lord? Are there still those who preach the Word of the Lord, the Bible, under the anointing of the Holy Spirit?

Many church leaders have reduced Sunday to a sermon about God and a service about us. God forgive us. And God forbid we gather for self-services and sermonettes about God. The church comes together each Sunday to meet with our God and Maker, enter His very presence, and behold His glory. We come to be touched by His hand and know the power of His Spirit. We come to hear the Word of the Lord for this people - His people - in this time and place. We come together to be transformed by the Word of God and His Holy Spirit.

Pastors, it's time you and I pay the price required to rightly call ourselves "preachers of the Word of God." It's time to pay the price in the study, rightly dividing the truth so what we preach in our pulpits is not our ideas about the Word of God, but God's word about Himself. It's time we pay the price on our knees, in holy desire to know Him as He is, not as we would have Him be. It's time we devote ourselves to prayer and the Word in tears of pastoral concern for people far from God, for the people whom God has entrusted to us, and for ourselves. In brokenness, let us declare to Him our deep need of His help as we dare to stand and preach God's Word to His people. Let us re-establish the study and prayer closet as personal upper rooms at the very heart of our souls and ministries.

Let us give ourselves to passionately seeking God in study, prayer, fasting, waiting, and even weeping before the Lord of Heaven and Earth (Psalm 126.5). Let us believe that every time we gather as His church, He will not merely visit us but will make His dwelling among us (II Corinthians 6.16). Let us anticipate that He will make us a living Upper Room of His glory and power (2 Acts 2.1-4)!

Let us trust He will be waiting for us every time we gather in His name, ready to make His Word come alive in our hearts. The Word that saves, heals, and sets captives free (Psalm 40.5)! The Word that makes our hearts burn within us as it reveals Jesus to us (Luke 24.32)! The Word that lovingly compels us to passionately go and do all He commands us to do (Matthew 28.20).

> *"Sermonettes and little talks on the subject of the Son of God? That will never do. What my heart longs for and what my soul is seeking is a Word from the Lord. I must know: is there any word from the Lord, a word of substance that sets my heart ablaze with its eternal freshness and life? Like the disciples on the road to Emmaus, I want my heart to burn within me every time I hear the preaching and teaching of the Word. And, God help me, my heart must burn within me every time I preach it."*
> *Le Prédicateur*[37]

---

[37] Journey Pastoral Coaching, Copyright © 2021

— Day 36 —

WHO WE ARE

*"And I will give you shepherds after my own heart, who will feed you
with knowledge and understanding." Jeremiah 3.25*

PENSÉE: IDENTITY

Pastor: păs'tər. (noun) Hebrew: ro`eh. Greek: poimēn. Definition: one
who tends, feeds, and defends God's sheep; one who provides
spiritual care to a body of believers; a shepherd.

Pastor. Before it can be a verb, it has to be a noun – only a pastor
can pastor. It's not just what we do; it's who we are. It is deeply
ingrained in our identity in Jesus Christ.

We wouldn't say a woman with children *does* mothering. Instead,
we rightly say she *is* a mother. It is her God-given creation and
calling. It is her heartbeat and breath. She's not a "birthing person"
or child care provider. She is a mother: she has a soul-level
connection with her children that defines her, them, and their
relationship. It's why she is willing to take on all the sacrifices that
come with being a mother. And she does so with joy. Not always with
happiness and dancing, but with deep-seated contentment and
satisfaction: "I am a mother; I am this child's mother. This is who I
am, so this is what I do."

Mother. It's so much more than what she does. It's who she is.
And so, being a mother defines and gives motivation for all she does.

In the same way, if not to the same degree, we do not *do* pastoring; we *are* pastors. It is our creation and call. It is our heartbeat and breath. We are not CEOs. We are pastors: we have a soul-level connection with people that defines us, our relationship with them, and yes, even them. It's why we are willing to take on the sacrifices that come with being a pastor. And with joy. Not always with happiness and dancing in the aisles, but with deep-seated contentment and satisfaction: "I am a pastor; I am this people's pastor. It's who I am, so it is what I do."

We know our sheep by name. They know our voice. Following the Great Good Shepherd, we lead them out to green pastures and still waters. They follow, even through the valley of the shadow of death. We have faith in them, and they trust us. We love them. They know we are not hirelings – this isn't a job we do. They know we are shepherds, pastors – this is who we are.

Pastor. It's so much more than what we do. It's who we are. And so, being pastors defines and gives motivation for all we do. Just like Jesus, the Great Good Shepherd.

> *"I'll always be a pastor even after I step down from this responsibility. I may not get paid then, and I may not be in charge of an organization, but I'll always have a pastoral concern for people. It's my call and my gift." Gordon MacDonald*[38]

---

[38] MacDonald, Going Deep p.95

— Day 37 —

THE GREATER PURPOSE

"Peter began to say to him, 'See, we have left everything and followed you.' Jesus said, 'Truly, I say to you, there is no one who has left house or brothers or sisters or mother or father or children or lands, for my sake and for the gospel, who will not receive a hundredfold now in this time, houses and brothers and sisters and mothers and children and lands, with persecutions, and in the age to come eternal life. But many who are first will be last, and the last first.'" Mark 10.28-31

PENSÉE: SACRIFICE

Often in Scripture and history, the narrative of the Church is told through the stories of pastors. The godly pastor pays a price, sometimes unthinkable, as he plays his part in the great unfolding work of the Gospel. He pays a price, often unbearable, as he answers God's call to pastor the people of God. And the story he helps write does not always produce a "feel-good" experience in his life. It comes at the cost of personal pain, sacrifice, and even loss.

But the faithful pastor continues on steadfastly, even relentlessly, because of God's call and His higher purposes. The mission of God and the love of Christ compel the godly shepherd to preach the Gospel, make disciples, provide pastoral care, and strengthen Christ's church. However pleasant or unpleasant the feelings or

103

"experiences," with blood, sweat, and tears, the pastor plays His part in God's story.

Why? Because there is a greater purpose to our calls than our personal feelings or "ministry experiences." As undershepherds, we serve at the pleasure of the Great Good Shepherd. We leave our homes, even our homelands, to fulfill His mission. Our heart is not to be celebrities or heroes in people's eyes, but to please the One who has called us. We live to see His glory magnified throughout the universe: it is Jesus who is the hero of the story! We are only undershepherds and storytellers, the ones to whom are given the privilege of presenting Him authentically to the church and world.

And for this greater purpose, we are gladly willing to pay whatever price He requires of us.

"For the Lamb that was slain! May He receive the reward of His suffering," was the cry of early Moravian missionaries on their way to their field of service. It remains the cry of every faithful pastor in our places of service today.

> *"When Joseph leaves home on this simple fact-finding mission, he leaves for the last time. Joseph will never return to live in the land until his bones are brought back after the Exodus (Ex. 13:19). In fact, it is this aspect of Joseph's story that warranted mention in the "Faith Hall of Fame" (Heb. 11:22). This is not a feel-good story wherein the hero returns victorious. This is a tale of redemption in which Joseph pays an unthinkable price for a purpose much greater than he." Voddie Baucham Jr.*[39]

---

[39] Taken from *Joseph and the Gospel of Many Colors* by Voddie Baucham Jr., (Wheaton: Crossway, 2013), p.52. Used by permission.

— Day 38 —

LIVING PARABLES OF JESUS

"So I exhort the elders among you, as a fellow elder and a witness of the sufferings of Christ, as well as a partaker in the glory that is going to be revealed: shepherd the flock of God that is among you, exercising oversight, not under compulsion, but willingly, as God would have you; not for shameful gain, but eagerly; not domineering over those in your charge, but being examples to the flock. And when the chief Shepherd appears, you will receive the unfading crown of glory." I Peter 5.1-4

PENSÉE: INFLUENCE

It was a Thursday afternoon. Someone was banging loudly on my front door, so I went to see who felt the need to knock down my house on my day off. Opening the door, I saw Mark (not his real name). Just a few months before, Mark had started attending our church youth group. He was an older teen, a loner, who had been invited by a friend that had recently joined our youth group and become a follower of Jesus. It was a story we saw repeated dozens of times in our ministry there – youth inviting friends to Jesus.

Mark was frantic. This was immediately clear. Anxiously looking up and down our residential street and reaching for the handle on my front door, Mark asked if he could come in. Seeing something was seriously wrong, I opened the door to him.

Standing in my living room, Mark reached his hands into the pockets of his jacket and pulled out multiple sandwich bags filled with drugs. He said he had been a dealer when he first came to church but had quit dealing since coming to Christ. This was good news. However, a friend had just called Mark's house that afternoon to warn him that someone had turned him in. The police were on their way to Mark's house at that moment to arrest him. Scared, Mark didn't know what to do or where to go, so he came to my house to ask for my help.

I won't go into the details, but simply say Mark took responsibility for his past actions and made his own decision to pay the price for what he had done. It turned out to be a smaller price because he voluntarily turned himself in to the police that day.

But this story is not about drugs or a drug dealer. Instead, it's a story about a brand-new child of God placing his very life in the hands of God even when he didn't know what that would mean. Still, as a new believer, he knew He could trust Jesus with his life and future.

And it's about a new child of God trusting God by turning to a pastor for help. Mark had known me for only a month, but something in his heart told him a pastor, his pastor, would stand by him and lead him in receiving God's help in redeeming not just his soul but his life. He trusted the man of God to help him get to the God of that man.

Pastor, you and I are not just "one of the guys." We are pastors. We are shepherds. We are living parables of Jesus Christ. When God's sheep can't see Him, hear Him, or sense Him near, they often see Him in us. And so, they come to us, trusting that, as undershepherds of Jesus, we will lead them to Him.

Let us walk among God's sheep as shepherds, living parables who reveal the Savior to them in all of His love and grace.

> *"Being a parable of Jesus Christ is an exceedingly powerful role." David Hansen*[40]

---

[40] Taken from *The Art of Pastoring* by David Hansen. (Downers Grove: IVP, 2012). p.144. Used by permission.

— Day 39 —

TRUE PASTORAL PRIVILEGE

*"For though you have countless guides in Christ, you do not have
many fathers. For I became your father in Christ Jesus
through the gospel." I Corinthians 4.15*

PENSÉE: GRATITUDE

"My pastor." I just got off the phone with a man I pastored almost 40
years ago. He's a pastor today. We've stayed in touch over the years,
talking ministry, family, the news of the day, and our life in Jesus.
It's been a relationship I've always treasured. Some calls are "How's
it going" catch-ups, and others are difficult conversations.

Today's call was a difficult one.

He called to give me the latest news on his father's cancer. He
called to tell me what he didn't want to say, and I didn't want to hear.
But he called to tell me the truth. And he called as an act of coming
to me, his pastor, for support. A pastor himself, he knows he needs a
pastor of his own. He knows he has one in me. What else could I be
with this great friend, this brother in Christ? Many years ago, God
knit our hearts together, and the connection has only grown deeper
over time, even though we are separated by far too much space.

Today, we talked about his dad's condition and prognosis. We
talked about the incredible man and friend his dad has been to so
many, including me. My friend and I talked about old times he and I

have shared and new times still ahead of us to create. We talked about our families, including the upcoming wedding of his only daughter. Words, laughter, tears, silence. And prayer.

As we said our goodbyes, he told me what he has told me so many times, "I just need to tell you how much I love you and thank God for you. I tell people all the time I wouldn't be who I am or even be in the ministry without you and your influence. We're friends, but you'll always be my pastor."

"My pastor." I'm still overwhelmed by this conversation. To think that as he faces one of the greatest sorrows he will ever know, followed so soon by one of the greatest joys he will ever experience, he needed and wanted to share them with me. He'll tell you he's had other wonderful pastors (to that, I can attest), but something between the two of us just clicked. Pastor for life. And friend for life.

Listen for it, Pastor. That quiet click in your heart that invites you into life-changing relationships with people. Some will let you in only so far, while others will throw the door wide open, giving you the privilege of doing life with them. Not just preaching to them, and not just pastoring them, but *being* their pastor. What a glorious place it is to be. What a humbling experience it is to know.

Don't force it, and don't even go looking for it. Just let it happen as you do life in Jesus with people. Relational clicks will come in smiles, thankyous, random phone calls, quiet conversations after church, an invitation to coffee, a backyard BBQ, Pastor Appreciation gifts, no-reason-at-all presents, and in one hundred and one other ways – moments when people come to their shepherd just to be with you. Why? Because in you, they sense the presence of the One they most need: the Great Good Shepherd, Jesus.

"My pastor." Never get over the privilege that is yours in being someone's pastor.

"I've never gotten over the humbling fact that, out of all the people in the world whom God could have called to be a pastor to His people, He called me." La Prédicateur[41]

---

[41] Journey Pastoral Coaching, Copyright © 2021

— Day 40 —

MORE

"You then, my child, be strengthened by the grace that is in Christ Jesus, and what you have heard from me in the presence of many witnesses entrust to faithful men, who will be able to teach others also. Share in suffering as a good soldier of Christ Jesus. No soldier gets entangled in civilian pursuits, since his aim is to please the one who enlisted him. An athlete is not crowned unless he competes according to the rules. It is the hard-working farmer who ought to have the first share of the crops. Think over what I say, for the Lord will give you understanding in everything. Remember Jesus Christ, risen from the dead." II Timothy 2.1-8

PENSÉE: TRUST

Once upon a time, churches were led and fed by shepherds. Today, many are directed and managed by CEOs. Once upon a time, pastors were qualified by their call, character, and anointing. Today they are considered qualified by their credentials, marketing skills, and ability to put bodies in seats.

But, Pastor, let us not sell our calls so easily. Even more, let us not sell our churches, our mission, or our Lord so cheaply.

A wise person said, "If God calls you to be a minister of the Gospel, don't stoop to be a king."

And don't stoop to be a businessman, even in shepherd's clothing.

We do not market the Gospel. We preach it, give it, and live it.

We do not put bodies in seats. We put souls in eternal fellowship with God and then provide watch-care to them throughout their lives. And for this, we shall one day give an account before the Great Good Shepherd (Hebrews 13.17).

We do not build organizations, even church ones. We make disciples, leaving the building of the church to the One who said this is His responsibility and guarantee (Matthew 16.18). Any organizing we do is of people and ministry, not businesses or brands. Jesus is our brand, and His Great Commission is our only business.

I am no businessman, and I refuse to become one.

I am a servant of the Most High King, the Lord of Heaven and Earth. I am His voice of life in a dying world, His teller of truth to His church. I am His undershepherd to the flock of His pasture, His own, His holy ones. I lead them to still waters and help them find and then rest in God's green pastures. I walk with them even through the very valley of the shadow of death. I work to see God's ongoing restoration, His renewal, in their souls. I lead them in the Great Mission of making disciples of Jesus Christ around the globe (Matthew 28-18-20).

I refuse the mantle of businessman. At the offer of any amount of money or promise of celebrity, I refuse it.

I am a minister of the Gospel of Jesus Christ.

"Once we're in active practice as ministers, we're handed ... job descriptions. Leadership and management principles drawn from the business world lie at the center of most of these alternate approaches, while others revolve around relational skills. Running a church becomes the focus rather than shepherding souls." Harold Senkbeil[42]

---

[42] Harold Senkbeil, p.116.

— *Post Script* —

A FILLED-UP SOUL

"On the last day of the feast, the great day, Jesus stood up and cried out, "If anyone thirsts, let him come to me and drink." John 7.27

Pastor, you owe your congregation a filled-up soul - a vine-abiding, Spirit-filled, grace-and-peace-overwhelmed, healthy soul.

If you're going to connect deeply with the Father on their behalf, you need a filled-up soul. If you're going to faithfully lead them to still waters and green pastures, you need a filled-up soul. If you're going to defend them against the enemies of their souls - wolves exterior and hirelings interior – you need a filled-up soul.

Even more, you owe God a healthy, vine-abiding, Spirit-filled, grace-and-peace-overwhelmed, healthy soul. If you want to live as His child instead of as a guest, you must live as a filled-up soul. If you want to live in the flow of His life instead of only occasionally tasting and seeing that He is good, you must live as a filled-up soul. If you want to know His truth and be set free daily by it, rather than living on a word here and there, you need a filled-up soul.

Spiritual dryness may fill the land and even ministers around you, but not you, Pastor. By the grace of God and at His personal invitation, you will enter into the Holy of Holies daily and abide there. Even deeper, you will abide in Him. You will know His refreshing, given you by His own heart and hand. You will know His confidence and power, breathed into you by His own Spirit.

You owe your congregation and God a filled-up soul. You will be a filled-up soul. Not because you or I say so, but because Jesus is even now working to make it so. Listen carefully, and you will hear His call: "If you are thirsty, come to me and drink." You have made the decision to respond and drink of Him fully.

You will give your congregation and God a filled-up soul.

"I owe my congregation a filled-up soul." Gordon MacDonald[43]

---

[43] A Resilient Life by Gordon MacDonald. (Nashville: Thomas Nelson, 2004). p.191. Used by permission.

REFERENCES

Anderson, Keith R and Randy D. Reece. *Spiritual Mentoring.* Downers Grove: InterVarsity Press, 1999.

Baucham Jr., Voddie. *Joseph and the Gospel of Many Colors.* Wheaton: Crossway, 2013.

Carson, D.A. *Memoirs of An Ordinary Pastor.* Wheaton: Crossway, 2008.

Challies, Tim. *Challies.com.* 25 September 2017.

Clinton, J. Robert. *The Mentor Handbook.* Altadeena, CA: Barnabas Publishers, 1991.

Billy Graham Evangelistic Association. billygraham.org

Hansen, David. *The Art of Pastoring.* Downers Grove: IVP, 2012.

Hodge, Charles. *A Commentary on the Epistle to the Ephesians.* Edinburgh: Banner of Truth, 1964.

M'Cheyne, Robert Murray. *Memoir and Remains of the Rev. Robert Murray M'Cheyne,* Ed. Andrew A. Bonar. Edinburgh: Banner of Truth, 1844.

MacDonald, Gordan. *A Resilient Life.* Nashville: Thomas Nelson, 2004.

MacDonald, Gordon. *Going Deep.* Nashville: Thomas Nelson, 2011.

Macy, Howard. *Rhythms of the Inner Life.* Old Tappan: Fleming H. Revell, 1988.

Marshall, Peter. *The Light and the Glory.* Old Tappan: Fleming H. Revell, 1980.

Maxwell, Chris. *Pause for Pastors.* Travelers Rest, SC: True Potential Inc, 2014. chrismaxwell.me

Morgan, G. Campbell. *This Was His Faith: The Expository Letters of G. Campbell Morgan.* Ed. Jill Morgan. Westwood: Revell, 1952.

Navajo, José Luis. *Mondays With My Old Pastor.* Nashville: Thomas Nelson, 2012. thomasnelson.com

Peterson, Eugene. *The Contemplative Pastor.* Grand Rapids; Wm. B. Eerdmans, 1989.

Peterson, Eugene. *The Pastor: A Memoir.* San Francisco: HarperOne, 2012. harperone.com

Sayers, Dorothy. *Letters to a Diminished Church: Passionate Arguments for the Relevance of Christian Doctrine.* Nashville: Thomas Nelson, 2004.

Senkbeil, Harold. *The Care of Souls.* Bellingham, WA: Lexham Press, 2019. lexhampress.com

Spurgeon, Charles. *Lectures to My Students.* Grand Rapids: Zondervan, 1977.

Spurgeon, Charles. *Morning and Evening.* Public domain.

Wells, David F. *No Place For Truth.* Grand Rapids: Wm. B. Eerdmans, 1993.

ABOUT JOURNEY PASTORAL COACHING

Studies demonstrate that one of the healthiest habits any minister can have is walking with a mentor or pastoral coach. This is especially true for young ministers. Journey Pastoral Coaching is dedicated to helping young ministers build strong for a lifetime of healthy and effective ministry. Yes, we help them survive, but more than that, we help them thrive.

While other great coaching ministries focus on leadership skills or church growth, Journey focuses on the minister him or herself. Doing flows from being, so we talk first and most about being. We're convinced that as we build the minister, we build the ministry – and we do so for a lifetime of healthy and effective ministry.

Journey's approach is unique. Our members walk with a mentor who helps them develop depth as they benefit from the wisdom that only comes through experience. But JPC is more than a regularly scheduled call with a mentor. It is a coaching community in which members invest in each other through peer calls, resourcing, and offering pastoral care to one other. Our members make Journey a "mutual investment ministry," one that yields huge dividends.

Journey's approach is also unique in that our members do not pay for coaching; they "earn" it. They earn it by investing in each other as described above. Why do we take an "earn your coaching" rather than a "pay for it" approach? There are three primary reasons.

First, young ministers most want and need pastoral coaching but can least afford the expense. The early years of ministry often include substantial student loan debt and entry-level salaries. So, rather than add to their burden, we remove it by providing mentorship and coaching without financial cost.

Second, churches served by young ministers can also find the cost prohibitive. While some churches are unwilling to invest in the lives and ministries of their young pastors, most churches want to steward them well but often do not have the financial resources.

Finally, the church at large faces a great leadership challenge in that the pulpit is aging at an alarming rate. Many young ministers find the stresses of vocational ministry overwhelming. Without the support of a mentor or coach, they give up and walk away. We at Journey believe God has called us to address this great need in the church.

By providing "no-financial-cost" coaching to young ministers, we believe we are providing a needed service to young pastors, local churches, and the church at large.

We at Journey are able to carry out our mission thanks to the faithful generosity of our partners, churches, and individuals like you who support Journey with prayer and finances each month or with special one-time gifts.

At Journey, we help young ministers build strong for a lifetime of healthy and effective ministry. We invite you to become a part of their success story by becoming a Journey Partner.

For more information, please visit our website.

JOURNEYPASTORALCOACHING.COM